AN ACT OF SURRENDER

Recover from Alcohol and Drug Addiction and

Be Happy, Joyous, and Free!

Order this book online at www.trafford.com
or email orders@trafford.com

Most Trafford titles are also available at major online book retailers.

Note for Librarians: A cataloguing record for this book is available from Library
and Archives Canada at www.collectionscanada.ca/amicus/index-e.html

Printed in Victoria, BC, Canada.

ISBN: 978-1-4251-8988-4 (sc)

ISBN: 978-1-4251-8990-7 (e-book)

*We at Trafford believe that it is the responsibility of us all, as both individuals and corporations,
to make choices that are environmentally and socially sound. You, in turn, are supporting this
responsible conduct each time you purchase a Trafford book, or make use of our publishing services.
To find out how you are helping, please visit www.trafford.com/responsiblepublishing.html*

*Our mission is to efficiently provide the world's finest, most comprehensive book publishing
service, enabling every author to experience success. To find out how to publish your book, your
way, and have it available worldwide, visit us online at www.trafford.com*

Trafford rev. 7/16/2009

North America & international
toll-free: 1 888 232 4444 (USA & Canada)
phone: 250 383 6864 ♦ fax: 250 383 6804 ♦ email: info@trafford.com

DEDICATION

to Jean Stimson (nee Nicolson)
whose steadfast faith allowed her
family to rise above the wounds
of addiction.

ACKNOWLEDGEMENTS

Numerous people contributed to this book in one way or another, and most certainly without their input and support it would surely not exist. First and foremost, Nancy would like to thank Ken Waldie who encouraged her from the very beginning to write this book with Jim. Ken's input draft after draft was indispensable. She also owes a big thank you to her daughter Morgaine who patiently allowed her mom on many evenings and weekends to spend countless hours in front of the computer when they could have been off having fun. Jim is most grateful to his wife Jan for her love and encouragement, allowing him to dig deeper within himself to share his story.

We both want to thank David Lee for designing the cover of the book, Dr. Ray Baker for offering to review the book, Doug Brown for suggesting the title, and Scott Hastings for doing such a nice job with the typesetting and book design. We have several people to thank for their suggestions and careful editing. They include Richard McDonald, Valerie Bruce, Nancy Blair, Chris Colero, and Jean Stimson. In addition, many others read various drafts of the book and provided valuable feedback. These people include Neal Berger, Jacquie Brandt, Sylvia Olsen, Ryan Stimson, Rob Stimson, Angie Brown, Ashley Stimson, Rob DeClark, Pastor Virgil Olson, Pastor Norm Botterill, James Drinkwater, Kathleen Landry, Lew F., Pastor John Nicholson and Lynn Nicholson, Bob DeClark, Chaplain Greg Darjes, Noel Coon (Dallas, Texas) and Peter Goodman (South Yorkshire, England).

CONTENTS

FOREWORD

For the past 25 years I've observed Jim Stimson in his role as an addictions professional helping countless addicts and family members—people who frequently came into his life in the most serendipitous of ways. Numerous times I was moved to tears as these individuals took his advice, did the work they needed to do, and turned their lives around.

It occurred to me one day that someone should capture Jim's stories and what I call his folksy wisdom in a book. I thought it would be wonderful if he were able to touch a greater number of people with his unique insights into what it takes to achieve recovery from addiction. It struck me that if a book was ever going to get written, that I should be the one to make it happen because he would probably frustrate the heck out of anyone else. I say that in the most loving, respectful way as anyone who knows Jim knows what a hectic, chaotic schedule he keeps.

When Jim agreed to write this book with me, I promptly devised a list of questions for him to answer into a tape recorder, which he usually did while driving somewhere. As I transcribed hours and hours of tape and listened to Jim bare his soul describing his childhood, his own escapades with drinking and using drugs, his relationships, his personal struggle to achieve true contentment, and his philosophy about life, I knew this book needed to be written. Jim's tapes were brimming with information to help people devastated by addiction, either their own or a loved one's, begin the healing process.

Jim has devoted his professional life to helping addicts and their families, as well as assisting workplaces and communities deal with the insidious problems created by substance use and abuse. But his unique perspective on drug addiction and recovery also comes from being raised in a home with an addicted father and struggling with his own 10-year addiction that began at the age of 15. In addition, Jim has done an enormous amount of personal and spiritual work over many years in his search to find his authentic self.

Working on this book with Jim has been one of the most rewarding experiences of my life. There is just so much valuable wisdom here for people who have been touched directly or indirectly by addiction. I am honored to be a part of bringing this book to life.

Nancy Lee
August 2009

PREFACE

I can honestly say that I had never given any thought to writing a book about my professional and personal life experiences and philosophy about addiction and recovery. However, when my dear friend and colleague Nancy Lee approached me about doing a book together, I realized that perhaps this was a way to offer some hope and a deeper understanding of addiction and recovery to a few more people than could otherwise be achieved in the course of my day-to-day life. A book would allow me to share what I have learned about this disease, how it impacts families, what recovery requires, and maybe a few of the pearls of wisdom I've picked up during my life's journey. It is my sincere desire that people will come to see that chemical addiction is a primary, progressive, and terminal illness that has a major negative impact, not only on the abuser, but also on the family. Addiction does not have to be a hopeless affliction, something best swept under the rug.

As a Registered Social Worker, I have an academic background in understanding addiction and recovery, but as someone who has worked in the profession for more than 30 years, I've seen a lot. Some of the most insightful teachings I received came from people with many years of recovery, some of whom had probably not completed high school. These professors of the school of hard knocks knew more about life—what works and what doesn't in the real world—than one could ever learn in school. I've been incredibly blessed to have had some amazing teachers and healers come into my life.

Looking back it was inevitable that I would start drinking and using drugs, and just as inevitable that I would end up spending my entire professional career—34 years and counting—working with addicts and families, as well as developing workplace and community-based counseling and intervention programs.

During my childhood I was constantly confronted with the conflicting messages of my father's excessive drinking and my mother's strong Christian values. Both got integrated into my developing psyche.

When I was nine, my mom sent my older brother Doug and me to live on her brother's farm in Raymore, Saskatchewan for a year when my father's drinking got really bad. After that I spent the next five summers there. This was a real 'Bible Belt' area of Canada and my relatives were evangelical Christians who believe that God's wrath would be visited upon those who sinned, and there were things you shouldn't do like drink alcohol, smoke, and gamble.

My time spent on the farm taught me about the spirit of community; whenever trouble befell any farmer in the area, neighbors were there in a heartbeat to help. I'm so grateful to my relatives who provided me with the opportunity to grow up with the simple, hard-working, and honest lifestyle of the prairies. It somehow balanced the chaos and turmoil created by my father's alcoholism and the hardships it caused my family. The values that I picked up helped me immeasurably in my work assisting addicts, families, workplaces, and communities deal with the scourge of substance abuse and addiction.

Addiction has a strong genetic component, and as life would have it, I ended up spending 10 years of my life as an alcoholic and drug addict, suffering many of the difficulties that go along with addiction. However, I feel blessed to have known the disease first hand because it allowed me to get inside my own heart, as well as the hearts of many people with whom I've worked, and be able to share some insights about this disease and what successful recovery requires.

This book is not intended to be my autobiography or a memoir, although it does talk about what my life was like growing up with an alcoholic father and my own addiction and recovery. I also share the stories of family members and a variety of clients from over the years (names have been changed to protect anonymity), in order to paint a picture of what drives the addict, what a life of recovery requires, and how to achieve contentment in life. Nancy and I both dug deep within ourselves and shared from our hearts what we believe it takes to enjoy a life that is what 12-step programs refer to as "happy, joyous, and free."

In fact we decided, after giving it considerable thought, to use this well-known phrase in the subtitle of the book because it captures so perfectly what we both believe our Higher Power wants for each one of us, not just those working on their recovery.

Throughout the book we make the point that recovery is not just about stopping drinking or using drugs, it's also about creating a life that is filled with love and hope, fun and laughter, harmony and balance, passion and connection, and free of worry and fear—in other words to be happy, joyous, and free.

Achieving this state, we believe, requires that we go on a spiritual journey—undertaking a process of surrendering our ego to a power greater than ourselves (we tend to use the terms Higher Power and God throughout the book but readers can substitute any term they wish that has a special meaning for them), in order to heal our spirit and find our authentic self.

It is my hope that by sharing stories and my beliefs about addiction and recovery, people will be inspired to look differently at their own alcohol and drug addiction-related issues, or those of a loved one, and take whatever action they need to in order to become more spiritually fulfilled and content with their life.

Jim Stimson
August 2009

CHAPTER ONE

℘

THE DEVASTATION OF ADDICTION

As human beings, our greatness lies not so much in being able to remake the world. . . as in being able to remake ourselves.

Mahatma Gandhi, 1869-1948, Political and Spiritual Leader

I woke up late in the morning with a feeling of defeat weighing heavy in my heart. Vague details of an accident the night before drifted through my consciousness—an argument in a bar, intentionally ramming a car broadside, spinning it out of my way, then speeding off down the road. I looked out my kitchen window to see my '67 Camaro parked in the backyard, the front grill smashed in. I had no recollection of driving home or if anyone had been hurt.

I told myself it didn't matter. I was fed up with life. I was fed up with me. I was fed up with being unhappy no matter what I did. I was fed up with living a hollow and empty life—a life controlled by booze and drugs. I was simply sick and tired of being sick and tired. I felt utterly and completely lost.

I glanced out the window again and saw a police officer walking around my car. I had no fear about what he might do to me, the fear that gripped me had everything to do with what was happening inside of me, in my addiction. The officer knocked on the door of the house where I lived with three drinking and drug-using buddies, and asked to speak with James Cameron Stimson.

"That's me." I invited him in.

"You were reported in a hit and run last night."

"Yes, I did that."

Sitting in one of the chairs stolen from our favorite drinking establishment, the officer wrote me up for leaving the scene of an accident. He could well have written me up for a hit-and-run, a much more serious charge.

Fortunately no one had been injured or killed. It was not my first drinking and driving offense, but it was my last. Something in me snapped that day. I realized that I didn't want my life to become my dad's life. I didn't want my addiction to hurt people the way his addiction had. I felt ashamed of what I had become, ashamed that my compulsion to use drugs was stronger than my own marriage vows. I had let down the people who meant the most to me: my mother, my wife, my family, my friends. I was unreliable, unfaithful, dishonest, selfish, and the list went on. These feelings pulled me down into a black abyss. I didn't feel that I belonged on this planet—I lived in a different place inside of myself, a place I didn't want anyone else to see.

But from the depth of my despair, a light flickered in the back of my mind. A voice in my head said, "Jim, you have to do something. You can't do it on your own. You have to reach out and get help." I recalled that Bill, a good friend of my father's, stopped drinking through a commitment to active involvement with other recovering alcoholics. I managed to get in touch with them. It was Saturday, February 19, 1972, the day that marks the beginning of my journey of recovery and transformation, a journey that continues to this day.

I don't know what I would have done if I hadn't known about Bill. That was the only meaningful piece of information I had about getting help. I had attempted to quit on numerous occasions, I'd even gone for counseling and taken Antabuse (a drug that induces vomiting if alcohol is consumed) in an effort to quit. I'd probably been told about recovery groups in the past, but my pride and ego had never let me hear it. Even more than that, I think that my feelings of guilt, shame, and remorse weighed me down so much that I had never wanted anyone to know who I was inside and what I had done.

For most of my life to that point I felt that I was never good enough—not as well educated, not as good looking, not as well dressed, not as capable—just not as good as anyone. On a few occasions I felt better than others, but I never felt equal to the people in my life. Of course, I never let people see that—I used every skill and ability I had to hide my insecurities. I projected an image of a guy who was reasonably in control, who did his job well, who kept to himself and didn't let people get too close. My whole heart and soul wanted to engage others, but I didn't know how to because I didn't know who I was. I don't ever recall up to that point in my life having a sense of my *self*. Instead, I would try to figure out what other people liked and who they wanted me to be so they would like me. In the end I was just phony, not real, and the more I pretended, the further I grew away from who I was deep inside.

Consequently I was driven by a profound sense of loneliness. I continued to drink and use drugs because I thought it would help me find the companionship that might fill the emptiness in me—maybe by being around people at parties, by trying to be the life of the party, I'd find the happiness I sought. I was never at peace, but desperately wanted to know it. I wanted to know how to love. Instead I just kept spiraling further downwards. I came to believe that alcohol and drugs were the only true friends I had, even though they eventually let me down. I was only 25 at the time and had been using alcohol and drugs for 10 years.

As I sit here today and reflect back on that time, I know without question that I'd rather be dead than live through that zombie-like existence again when I was spiritually and emotionally bankrupt. But when you grow up in a dysfunctional home, and don't receive the fullness of love and nurturing that all children should receive, you are missing something that is critical to feeling whole and complete. And when you add years of addiction on top of that, any possibility of living a happy, meaningful, and fulfilled life is hijacked. It would take me many years of actively working on my recovery to feel whole again.

CUMULATIVE DEVASTATION

The damage wrought by addiction is beyond calculation. The families of addicts pay an enormous emotional toll. In my family my father was an alcoholic and three of my four siblings became addicts. My only sister died of an overdose, as did a cousin and a niece. Five of our relatives were killed by drunk drivers in three separate collisions. More recently, one of my two sons, a niece, and a nephew were treated for addiction—all are in their twenties.

There is no doubt that the toll addiction takes on individuals, their families, and the communities they live in, is a cumulative devastation that has a widespread ripple effect. Substance abuse is associated with vehicle accidents, domestic violence, child abuse, suicides, crimes such as rape, aggravated assault, robbery, and larceny, and with costly social and public health problems such as HIV/AIDS and fetal alcohol syndrome. For young people it is also associated with teen pregnancy and failure in school.

How can we even begin to calculate the social, economic, and even spiritual harm that is done? On top of all this, what is the cost of lost productivity to our workplaces, or the increased costs for law enforcement and on our legal and social systems? And how about direct and indirect healthcare costs? I've seen statistics that say the financial burden is in the billions. But the dollar value pales in light of the true human cost—the suffering of bereaved families and friends.

It saddens me, after decades in the substance abuse field, to see that drug use and abuse are getting worse, not better. The quantity and potency of the drugs available on the street now are greater than ever. We increasingly find cocaine being used on the job. Prescription drugs, according to some addicts I know, are easier to purchase on the street than in a pharmacy. Television commercials show our youth how they can have a good time if they just drink the *right* beer.

It is not unheard of these days for children as young as 10 or 11 to start using illicit drugs or alcohol. Where substance use dependence was once thought to be an adult-onset disease, it is now being called a "developmental disease" because it generally starts during adolescence and even childhood. There is a clear correlation between the age people first use drugs or alcohol, and their potential for developing a serious problem later on.

Over the long-term, the implications of substance abuse and addiction are staggering, yet not nearly enough is being done. We certainly don't see people out raising money for addiction treatment and research like we see for heart disease or cancer. This is largely because so many people persist in seeing addiction as the product of weak people making poor choices. But the fact is, there is a point in the progression of the disease where the user loses control over his or her ability to say no. Because of misunderstanding and lack of education regarding substance abuse, we are losing ground on the societal recognition of addiction being an illness. And it *is* a disease. Using brain imaging scans, medical researchers can now prove that it is a disease of the brain.

WASTED LIVES

Drug and alcohol addictions destroy lives. Few people will argue with this because we all have a mental image of hardcore drunks or druggies living on skid row. But only a small percentage of alcoholics and addicts end up living on the street. Seventy-five percent of addicts are in the workforce. These people continue to hold down jobs and live with their families, sometimes not realizing they are chemically dependent. As their illness progresses they will do whatever it takes to hold onto their jobs, even long after their families have left them.

Unfortunately, many people who are chemically dependent don't get noticed because society does not see, or chooses not to see, the problems these people cause. And those who do get noticed often do so because they are in late stage dependency. I've worked with many professionals and executives who are high functioning addicts, and from the outside their lives appear to be normal. But inside, they are often increasingly unhappy people who make life miserable for their family.

While much of the devastation caused by addiction is obvious—accidents, crime, violence, abuse—most of the harm it causes is very subtle as it plays out quietly in people's lives. Until something happens, for instance a fatal car accident, society pays little attention. We might get angry if an innocent person is injured, but we are indifferent to the problems of the addict. If people want to drink themselves to sleep every night, or snort cocaine in the comfort of their own home, then that is their prerogative.

Just to clarify, there are people who can drink on a daily basis but are not addicts. As explained in the following chapter, there is a point in time (which varies for each addict) when the drinking or using becomes an all-consuming obsession. Addiction is a progressive disease and for some people, it may be years before the disease really takes over and dominates their lives—for others it is almost immediate.

For many addicts, all that matters is the next drink or drug fix. It preoccupies their thinking. They become extremely self-centered, selfish, irresponsible, emotionally unavailable, and with time, completely withdrawn. It saps them of all zest for life, often leaving them feeling angry and frustrated with themselves and everyone around them. Prolonged use erodes their self control and ability to make sound decisions. They can have difficulty remembering, develop poor social behaviors, and their work performance and personal relationships suffer. Continued alcohol and drug use inevitably takes a toll on their physical and mental health. The majority of all addicts die younger than they should because of their addiction, either from medical complications, accidents, violence, or other causes related to their addiction.

CONNECTING THE DOTS

Often emotional damage inflicted on an addict's loved ones is not recognized or acknowledged until there is a crisis. Joanne, a recent acquaintance, was diagnosed with breast cancer, despite being a very health-conscious individual. Her doctor informed her that the cancer was not genetic, nor related to lifestyle choices, but was most likely a result of stress.

The cancer forced Joanne to take a close look at her life. She finally admitted to herself that after 38 years of living with an active alcoholic, life had become intolerable. Until this point, she had not been willing to acknowledge how desperately unhappy she was. Her husband had held different jobs over the years, but as his drinking progressed, he had difficulty staying employed. She worked hard to keep their family life together, and despite all this, she tended to blame herself for the problems in the marriage.

As family members often do, Joanne had learned to tolerate her husband's addiction, but by internalizing her anger and frustration, she created an environment in her body for the cancer to take hold. I informed Joanne that, in fact, her cancer may well be related to lifestyle choices—that choosing to stay in a relationship with an alcoholic for 38 years and not confronting it, was a lifestyle choice. At any time during those years she could have made a decision to do something about the situation (perhaps getting professional help or joining a support group). But as is often the case with addiction, family members can't separate themselves from the illness. They end up with their own feelings of guilt, shame, and remorse, believing that they contributed to it, and there is nothing they can do.

How many people like Joanne are there in the world today? How many family members get sick, perhaps even die, and they never connect the dots to see what made them unhealthy in the first place? Much of the time family members suffer far more than addicts, who continue to self-medicate, unaware of the devastation they are inflicting upon their loved ones.

And then there are the children. There are many functioning addicts who come home from work each day and proceed to drink or use drugs, perhaps hiding it from their children, or even worse, engaging them in its use. When it comes time for everyday activities like putting a healthy meal on the table, or helping children with their homework, or tucking them into bed, addicted parents just aren't available. In so many subtle ways, the child is neglected, emotionally abused, and robbed of a healthy, nurturing family life, and the stage is set for the next generation of drug abusers. It may not be until these children are well into their adult lives that they connect the dots and come to realize how being raised in the home of an addict impaired their ability to attract, develop, and maintain deep, meaningful, loving and mutually rewarding relationships.

MY DAD AND ME

I grew up with an alcoholic father who was usually able to remain employed, despite losing or quitting numerous jobs. He was a heavy duty mechanic and his skills were always in demand. While I grew up knowing that I was loved by both my father and my mother, Dad's drinking wrecked havoc on our household and the whole family paid a heavy price.

My dad's drinking really took off when I was in elementary school. Dad often worked out of town at different construction camps and when he was home he'd usually go out mid-afternoon, not to return until after midnight. As a boy of eight I came to anticipate his routine, so when he was not working away from home, I would force myself to lie awake and wait for him. When he'd stumble in, I'd watch him from behind the slightly ajar bedroom door. Quite often he would sit in front of our old Spartan record player and listen to "The Day Jimmy Brown Got Married" or "The Shifting Whispering Sands." As a child I could not begin to comprehend what that was about. Years later I understood that he was wallowing on the pity pot of life feeling sorry for himself.

Often he would start crying, and then either go to sleep, or else wake up my mom and start an argument with her. That was what I dreaded most. I got to know intuitively at what level of intensity the argument should reach before I needed to insert myself. By this time I was sobbing uncontrollably and my presence, as I knew it would, always put an end to the argument. All I wanted was for it to stop. I don't remember being scared for me, but rather for my mom. I'd never seen him hit her, but dishes did fly at times. My mom held the family together and if she had been injured, I don't know what would have happened to us.

This whole experience left me, an eight-year old little boy, feeling exhausted and relieved, but more importantly, with an ever-increasing sense that it was my responsibility to put a stop to my parents' arguments. Addicts, in the selfishness of their disease, don't comprehend the degree of emotional pain and damage they inflict on young children, and how they deprive them of the right to a happy, carefree childhood. It is impossible to estimate how many children today live with similar experiences every day.

When I was 12, I remember going to a hockey league father-son banquet. My dad had promised he would be there but went out drinking instead. I remember feeling physically sick with a sense of overwhelming loneliness, thinking that I must be the only boy there without his father. I have a vivid memory of myself in that banquet room, surrounded by people, but feeling so very alone. One of the greatest harms addicts inflict on their children is simply not being present and involved in their lives. Another is to be physically present, but a source of embarrassment or shame.

Often on a Saturday afternoon when Dad was in town I would tag along when he went drinking at the Legion or Army and Navy Club. I would wait outside in the old '47 Chevy and page him every 30 minutes or so. He'd eventually show up at the door, give me 35 cents, enough for a bottle of Coke and an Oh Henry chocolate bar, and then head back inside. I am sure my mother encouraged me to tag along as it got one of the five kids out from under her feet, and it also meant Dad would have to return home earlier than if he did not have a child in his care.

I always thought those Cokes and chocolate bars were the reason for my going along. It was not until I was in my 50's, standing in a friend's kitchen talking about my dad, that with an unexpected flow of tears, I fully realized that the Cokes and Oh Henrys meant nothing to the child I was then. I went because I loved my dad dearly, and I had to work with his alcoholism just to have a few minutes of his time. At that moment, I felt so thankful that my two sons did not grow up during my active addiction.

MY YEARS AS AN ADDICT

For years I held hope in my heart that Dad would miraculously come to his senses, stop drinking, and again become the kind, loving man he was when I was a very young boy. I hoped that somehow his union or his employer would give him some sort of ultimatum. Or, that the police would pick him up and lock him away. Or, he'd get hurt and end up in hospital or a mental institution. I even reached the point where I hoped that he would die. It's not unusual for children to wish their addicted parent would die and put an end to everyone's misery. I didn't know back then, that with the right knowledge and support, there is always hope that addicts like my father can recover.

When I was 16, I couldn't take it any longer and decided to go stay with my relatives on their farm in Raymore, Saskatchewan where I'd spent many summers. I planned to tell no one, not even my mother, that I was leaving that day. I cleaned out my school locker and went home to get my things.

Mom happened to be home, so with tears rolling down my cheeks, I ended up telling her I was leaving home for good and heading for Raymore. She was heart-broken, not just by this, but by the fact it represented what our home life had become because of Dad's alcoholism. She knew intuitively she needed to release me with love. We didn't know what the years ahead held in store, but little did we know that the scene that day as I left home was akin to the parable of the Prodigal Son.

I arrived unannounced at my relative's farm and they took me in asking few questions. I enrolled at school to complete grade 10. It wasn't long before I started drinking—my cousin Jim and I took it up together and we got into more than our share of trouble.

A month before final exams, the two of us borrowed my aunt's brand new 1963 Pontiac Laurentian to go to a wedding in the neighboring town of Lestock. On our way home, near midnight, just outside of Lestock, a car with its headlights off came up over a hill, driving halfway over the center line, and hit us head on.

There were three of us in the front seat, my cousin driving, our buddy in the middle, and me in the passenger seat. Of the three of us, I'd had way too much to drink. Seconds before the collision my head was hanging out the window for some fresh air, my neck was resting against the post for the vent window. My cousin asked me to close the window and as I sat back in my seat we were hit. If I hadn't moved I would have been decapitated.

Not wearing a seat belt my head careened off the dash and went through the windshield. I somehow managed to pull free, open the door, and scramble out of the car. I learned later that despite massive bleeding, I stumbled through a ditch, crawled through a four-strand barbed-wire fence, and started running across a field. I don't know how far I ran before I collapsed as if I'd run into a brick wall. Fortunately, a friend Gary and his girlfriend were following in his pickup truck and he spotted me leaving the wreck and head into the ditch. If he'd been traveling behind us even 30 seconds later and missed seeing me, I would have bled to death in that Saskatchewan summer fallow field.

I remember brief moments of consciousness in Gary's truck knowing I was in serious condition. In the hospital, I recall being told that the attending doctor determined that I had lost so much blood that he would neither freeze my deep facial cuts, nor put me under. I was strapped to the operating table as the medical staff stitched my head wounds back together. I would pass out and come to over and over again under the intensity of the operating lights.

At one point I recall asking the doctor if he believed in God. He said he did and I responded that I did too. Then I passed out once more. The hospital used up every available ounce of my blood type and gave me 24 hours to live or die. Amazingly I was released 48 hours later. No one could believe the speed of my recovery. My brush with death was not enough, however, to deter me from carrying on drinking.

While I was in the hospital, I went to the room of the older man who had hit us. I ended up talking with him and playing a few games of cribbage. I don't remember who won, but I do remember that in some way he reminded me of my father. I expect that this man too was an alcoholic, I just didn't know or understand it then. I went home to the farm and shortly after wrote my final exams for grade 10.

I quit school that year and proceeded to drift from job to job. More and more, drinking became a part of my life. I worked hard, played hard, and drank hard. Like most addicts, I did a lot of foolish things.

When I was 18, I walked a mile or so in a drunken stupor to the wedding celebration of an ex-girlfriend. It was the middle of winter with sub-zero temperatures, and I wasn't even wearing shoes. The guests at the wedding party called the town cop who escorted me to a two-cell jail in Raymore. My toes were badly frost-bitten, but fortunately for me the fellow on duty at the jail had been in a prisoner of war camp and he knew that in order to save my feet, he should rub them with snow. After rubbing my feet for an hour and a half, he was so tired he said he wanted to nap on the cot in the jail cell and leave me out at the desk. He asked me to wake him up just before the police were supposed to arrive to charge me so I could get back in the cell.

Another time in High Prairie, Alberta I took my landlord's truck while he was away so I could get to a party out in the bush. On the way back the police had set up a routine road check. One of the officers stepped out to stop me but had to dive out of the way because I kept on going. They caught me as I pulled into the yard. I woke up in jail the next morning with no idea how I got there, not remembering anything of the night before.

I started to suffer blackouts the day I started drinking, although generally they are a definite sign of the progression of alcoholism. I didn't know that—I just figured if you bought booze and drank it, forgetting what happened during the course of the night was part of the deal. Throughout 10 years of drinking I rarely remembered much of what occurred when I was drunk. I had to piece together what happened the night before by using questions and humor with my friends who had been with me.

Anyway, I was charged with impaired driving. When it was time to go to court, I didn't want to go. My boss Joey was a good guy and agreed to attend in my place so I could operate the loader that day. It cost me my license for six months and a $600 fine—pretty stiff in those days. I was so steamed, I told Joey I wouldn't let him go to court for me ever again because I was sure that I could have gotten off with a lighter sentence. It didn't occur to me that the real issue was that I had an alcohol and drug problem.

Another time while visiting friends in Vancouver, I was so drunk after a party that when I tried to drive out of an underground parking garage, I kept hitting other parked cars and someone phoned the police. Apparently, I got into an argument with one of the officers and was placed in solitary confinement in the Vancouver City Jail—a tiny windowless cell with a urinal, sink, and mat on the floor. When I came to I found I'd been stripped down to my underwear, and once again had no recollection of what had happened the night before. The sheer terror of not knowing if I had killed someone nauseated me. The charge of just being drunk and disorderly was actually a relief.

At six in the morning they moved me to the drunk-tank, a real nasty place where they served a steamed and putrid-smelling meal on old pewter plates. It was too disgusting for me to eat, but when I put the plate down three guys grabbed it. Again, the humiliation of the experience didn't penetrate my consciousness, nor put me off drinking.

When I was 22, I went back to school and worked on my grade 12 adult upgrading at Alberta College in Edmonton. I was still drinking, and now doing drugs, mostly marijuana, but also hash, acid, speed, MDA, and mescaline. I completed my adult upgrading and enrolled in a business and marketing course at the Northern Alberta Institute of Technology. By the end of the first year, I was failing badly due to alcohol and drug use, so I switched into the two-year Social Services Technology course.

Wanting to be accepted, I got involved with school council, ended up as student vice-president, and participated in a variety of school activities. In my last year, I ran for president of the students' association, but blew any chance of winning when I got drunk and made a fool of myself on stage at the school's annual Santa's Anonymous Christmas fund-raising event (which I'd helped organized). Understandably, I lost all credibility and did not get elected.

While attending college, I met and married Sylvia. I kept my drinking and drug habits carefully hidden from her until the day I put her wedding ring on. It was no surprise my marriage was soon in real trouble. Before the end of my last year of school, in our fourth year of marriage, Sylvia laid down the law. She told me we were going for counseling and she'd already lined us up with a therapist.

On our first and only visit, the therapist initiated the conversation asking, "Why are you here?"

Sylvia replied, "Jim has a drinking problem."

"Is this true?" he asked me.

"No, I only drink on weekends."

"Sylvia, does Jim's drinking affect the relationship?"

"Absolutely!"

"Did you hear that?" the therapist asked me.

"Yeah, but I don't drink any more than the guys I hang out with," I responded belligerently.

"Sylvia, if Jim continues with his drinking, what will you do?"

"Leave him."

"Did you hear that?" he asked again.

"Yeah, but I don't have a drinking problem, there may be some issues, but there is no need for me to quit."

He turned to Sylvia and said, "Well Mrs. Stimson, our session is over and I suggest you follow through on what you need to do in your life."

And he left us. I was so angry, but looking back I totally respect his straightforwardness and his understanding of the selfishness of the disease. Sylvia did leave me.

Numerous times during the unravelling of my marriage I would get drunk or stoned and drive to my parents' place. I would sit on the edge of my mom's bed and cry because I knew my life was not what I wanted it to be. At that time, Mom knew little about addiction or recovery, and she could see I was following in my dad's footsteps, but all she could do for me was to pray. Looking back, I believe this was the best thing she could have done.

February 19,1972, eight months after Sylvia left, I had my hit-and-run at the age of 25. I 'hit bottom' and gave up drinking and using. With a tremendous amount of support, and a lot of effort on my part, I've remained clean and sober to this day.

CHAPTER TWO

&

UNDERSTANDING THE ADDICT

Seek not to understand that you may believe, but believe that you may understand.

Saint Augustine, 354-430, Theologian

The first time I had an understanding of addiction in relation to social drinking was at an addiction conference early in my recovery. A medical doctor from Seattle offered the best explanation of social-versus-addictive drinking I have ever heard. He said, "Imagine you were to go to someone's house for a social gathering, and the hostess came around with a beautiful bowl of polished red apples offering them to each of the guests. You decide to take one. Sweet and juicy and delicious, you eat it gradually and savor every mouthful. If the hostess came back a short while later and asked if you would like another one, you would likely say, "No thank you, that was great, it hit the spot. I'm fine for now but maybe I'll have another one later in the evening."

The doctor asked, "Can you understand if you did that with alcohol? Those people are social drinkers—they can eat an 'apple' and stop after they have had just one."

As an addict, I would make sure I had brought my own apples to the party. And I'd have stashed some in the glove box, and under the seat, and in the trunk of my car. I would have had a couple of apples before going to this party. When I was at their house, if they didn't come around and offer more apples, I'd be getting up and helping myself, or offer to be at the apple bar and help distribute the apples myself. I would eat apples until they were all gone, and then I'd ask if they wanted me to get more, offering to throw in some money.

If I were hosting the party, I'd make sure to hide a couple of apples to protect my supply, so I would not find myself without later on or in the morning. Problem was, however, I would not be able to remember the next day where I hid them.

I have never been a social drinker—the concept of social drinking was beyond my comprehension. When I went out to drink, it was not always with the intention of getting drunk, but once I had a drink, I usually drank until I was drunk. I used to say, "I'm a social drinker" because anytime someone said, "I'm going to have a drink," I would say, "So shall I!"

CHRONIC, PROGRESSIVE, AND FATAL

The term addiction goes back to the 16th century where it was used to refer to the bondage of a servant to a master. Over time, the term came to describe a practice or habit that could not be broken. In both cases, it implied a loss of liberty of action. It was not until the beginning of the 20th century that the term was used to mean a habitual or excessive use of a drug, where the person could not voluntarily stop once they had started. It was understood that obtaining and using the substance dominated such a person's life.

I am one of those people who believe unequivocally that addiction is an illness, although there are numerous people who will argue otherwise. The American Medical Association first acknowledged alcoholism as a disease in 1956. In 1960, E.M. Jellinek, in his book *The Disease Concept of Alcoholism,* described alcoholism as chronic, progressive and if unchecked, fatal.

I have attended funerals for many people whose lives ended much too early because of addictive lifestyles. There is no question that the probable outcome for people who continue to abuse alcohol or drugs—legal or illegal—is premature death, including accidents, homicides, suicides, and of course, physical or mental illness.

Addiction as a disease is no different than cancer or heart disease, in that there are identifiable symptoms that do not respect race, sex, age, or economic status. Like cancer and heart disease, addiction is clearly influenced by genetic markers and tends to run in families. Researchers tell us that in families where one parent or grandparent is addicted, four out of seven family members can themselves develop an addiction. In my family, four of the five of us kids became addicts.

Some people believe that addiction is learned behavior—that children who grow up with an addicted parent/caregiver end up abusing drugs or alcohol because that's what they know. I grew up with an alcoholic father, and believe me, there was no way I wanted to end up like him. In my case, I thought I could have a few drinks with my friends now and again, but it wasn't long before I lost control over my ability to stop.

It baffles me that some people still see addiction as a case of missing willpower on a grand scale, arguing that addiction is self-inflicted. Yet cancer and heart disease each carry a significant measure of self-infliction through behavior and lifestyle choices such as smoking, sunbathing, poor diet, being overweight, and other environmental conditions within a person's control. While it is true that one must drink to develop alcoholism, there is no evidence that drinking causes alcoholism, nor does taking drugs causes drug addiction. I believe a combination of genetics and social/environmental factors are at the source of addiction.

It's important to clarify that there is a difference between becoming dependent on a substance (or activity) and suffering from the disease of alcoholism and addiction. For example, if we were to give drugs, let's say cocaine, to a group of people everyday for a period of time, they would all become physically addicted. In other words, they would all suffer withdrawal symptoms as they came off this drug. However, a percentage, some experts say one in seven, would not be able to remain drug-free after this—they'd be hooked, wanting more and more. It would take some kind of intervention for them to eventually stop.

One of the most succinct descriptions of the progression of alcoholism was written by the American novelist F. Scott Fitzgerald (1896-1940), himself an alcoholic: *"First you take a drink, then the drink takes a drink, then the drink takes you."*

Years ago I was fortunate to spend time with Father Martin, a Catholic priest and addiction specialist in the U.S. He would tell people that *if you are to understand addiction and the addict, you need to understand this one simple truth, and if you don't, you won't be able to understand or help them: the addict uses the drug that they use, in the way that they use it, when they use it, because they cannot use it in any other way.*

Both Father Martin and Fitzgerald are saying that alcoholics and drug addicts don't own the illness, the illness owns them. So of course they can't do it any other way, and of course they may do inappropriate things like lie, cheat, or steal. And they usually do this to the people in their life they love, or should love the most, which makes their actions all the more painful and disheartening. Addicts do things that they should never do—some are criminal acts, some are absolutely morally inappropriate, all are totally selfish and devastating for loved ones. In fact, I've heard it said that the 'i.s.m.' in alcoholism stands for 'I,' 'self,' and 'me.'

Another analogy I use to help people understand the addict is that we all have a pilot light burning within us. But for a percentage of people, based on genetics and background, early on that pilot light becomes a flame, ignited by alcohol or drugs, or even some activity like sex, gambling, or overeating. After that it never goes back to being just a pilot light, back to 'normal.' The experience of the pilot light being ignited can be quite a profound experience. Consequently, addicts are always looking to repeat it, and will continue to pursue that feeling despite negative consequences. That profound experience is unique to the addict, and is generally not available to those who are not predisposed to addiction.

Research has shown that individuals who are susceptible to addiction differ considerably in how easily and quickly they lose control over what was initially voluntary behavior. At some point, addicts move into a different state of being where they no longer have control over their drinking or drug use and continue despite increasing negative consequences. The disease of addiction has taken hold and life for them will never be the same. Dr. Ray Baker, an addiction specialist in Vancouver, likes to say that you can turn a cucumber into a pickle, but you can never turn a pickle back into a cucumber.

CUNNING, BAFFLING, AND POWERFUL

Many professionals in the bio-medical community today consider addiction to be a brain disease caused by persistent changes in brain structure and function. They say it is a disease that has inseparable biological and behavioral components. They also say that the disease-ravaged brain of a compulsive drug user resembles that of people with other kinds of brain diseases.

Having a disease of the brain does not absolve anyone from having to take responsibility for their harmful or hurtful behaviors, but it does explain why many addicts cannot simply stop and stay stopped by using sheer force of will. It also provides some insights into why they do some of the bizarre things they do.

When my dad was drinking and taking various prescription drugs towards the end of his active addiction, he would leave partially empty pill bottles out and a note saying he had overdosed, that his life wasn't working, and he was ending it. At first, we'd call an ambulance not knowing if he *had* overdosed. It was horrifying and frustrating because it happened on a number of occasions. This was early in my recovery when I had moved home for a short while.

I remember times driving home feeling terrified, not knowing if my father would be alive or dead. The closer I got, the more intense the anxiety got. I just wanted to turn around and go anywhere else. My family eventually got to the point where we didn't respond to his actions anymore. To my knowledge, he never did overdose, but what was this all about? Obviously a huge cry for help, but how confusing and painful for a family caught in the middle of such craziness.

"Cunning, baffling, and powerful" is how one recovery program describes the power of addiction, and there aren't three better descriptors. Whether you just see it, live with it, work with it, or are personally affected by it, you can clearly see how this description aptly explains the behaviors of addicts. Addiction is an illness where the affected individuals have the unique and continued capacity to forget all of the negative stuff that they caused, as well as what has happened to them.

As a result they only remember the positive times, which were actually few and far between, and therefore they can carry on unfazed.

Addicts do not set out with an intent to cause trouble or hurt the people they love. They desperately struggle to be the person they were before their addiction, or the person they would wish to be. They usually can't make sense of their own actions and reactions. Unfortunately, as addiction progresses and tightens its grip, the problems increase. Their increasing guilt, shame, and remorse in turn gives them cause to drink or use more, creating a vicious downward spiral.

As the disease progresses, it becomes more and more obvious to everyone. Addicts may start hanging out with different groups of friends, their appearance often becomes more disheveled, they become more emotional—grumpy, angry, jealous—and stay emotionally distant to protect themselves. They may move from job to job, community to community, relationship to relationship, all because of their addiction. Their desire is to stay private and escape, but addicts can't escape because wherever they go, there they are.

After a time it is no longer a question of starting out from a normal state when drinking or using drugs to feel euphoric, but increasingly from a state of remorse, guilt, or shame, in the hopes of feeling normal again. When I drank, I didn't come back to feeling normal, I came back to feeling guilty or ashamed about something that might have happened on my last drinking episode. I didn't even know at the time if maybe I'd hurt or misused a friend or loved one, or perhaps stolen something. I'd feel more and more remorse until I no longer drank from normal to feel good, I drank from remorse in an attempt to feel accepted and included, numb the pain, and feel some semblance of normal.

THE THREE "C'S" OF ADDICTION

Addiction literature talks about the three "C's" of addiction that are the key criteria for a diagnosis of this illness: compulsive using, control (or loss of), and consequences (continuing to use despite mounting negative outcomes).

As described with the analogy of the apple at the beginning of the chapter, the addict becomes preoccupied with the acquisition of, the ingestion of, and the effect of the substance. It could be alcohol, an illegal street drug, or a prescription or over-the-counter drug, and more often than not, some combination of these. As mentioned earlier, some activities such as sex, eating, shopping, and gambling can also be addictive and equally as destructive. [The focus of this book, however, is alcohol and drug addictions.] Using or drinking becomes the center or focal point of the addict's life—it's what matters most.

Compulsive use implies that someone has lost the ability to say "no." That is the nature of the disease—the illness owns them, they don't own the illness. I find it interesting that research in recent years looking at the brain in relation to addiction has confirmed what many of us in the field have long believed—repeated drug use changes the brain in fundamental and long-lasting ways. These changes to the brain then get translated over time into changes in behavior.

For some people, drugs and alcohol essentially hijack the brain's motivational control circuits so that drug use becomes the primary preoccupation of the addict. In other words, addicts develop a compulsive craving for the drug that controls their behavior, even in the face of significant negative health and social consequences.

When we talk about loss of control, there are three aspects: the amount, the timing or frequency, and the outcomes that result from their actions. Addicts may lose any one or some combination of these at different times. To illustrate this, let's say we have a father who is an active cocaine user who promises to be home on time for his daughter's birthday. He might even have bought a present in advance and be looking forward to the event. On that day, however, he feels compelled to stop off at his dealer. But he can't just do a single line of coke and he ends up being there for a much longer period of time. The addict may phone the family out of guilt or a derailed sense of obligation, but inevitably a big blow up takes place. The man knows it is his responsibility as a parent to be at his child's birthday party, but because he is driven by his addiction he loses control of all three aspects: the amount, the timing, and the consequences.

The issue of control is a real paradox for addicts. While they continually lose control over frequency, amount, and consequences, their deeper motivation is always to be in control of the situation. In order to do this, they become absolute masters of manipulation, lies, and deception, especially when it comes to creating occasions to drink or do drugs. Addicts are always setting up their schedules, ensuring there will be opportunities to use before, during, and after an activity, even arranging days off in order to have unobstructed access to their drug.

I was no different. While working on highway construction, I learned to pop the hydraulic lines of the John Deere tractor pulling a packer that I operated, effectively putting it out of commission for the rest of the day. I would never pop the hose before lunch, but always just after so the supervisor would have to shut my unit down for the day. I'd be sent home with full pay while the mechanics fixed the problem. The remainder of my day would then be spent at the 'zoo,' the nickname for the beer parlor at my favorite hotel. I must have popped that hydraulic line at least a half dozen times, always on a hot day.

My dad, like all addicts, lied and manipulated and kept his family at bay, all to make sure he had access to alcohol, his prescription drugs, and his lifestyle. Addicts do everything possible to keep the drug dealer or the bootlegger paid before anyone else because that is their access to their drug of choice.

In the later years of his addiction, when his marriage was in trouble, Dad manipulated three separate doctors to prescribe Valium, Librium, and Demerol. Being several months clean and sober at this time, I decided to meet with one of his doctors. It took many attempts for me to get an appointment, but when I did, I brought with me as many of the prescription bottles as I could find and asked the doctor what he thought he was treating my father for. He replied, "Depression and stress. I know your dad is going through a break-up with your mother."

I said, "Did you know that you are treating an active alcoholic? And do you know you are unknowingly contributing to his addiction and his breakup?" I then set up all the pill bottles in front of him and said, "Here is what he is getting from this doctor, and here's what he gets from that doctor, and on top of that he goes to the local hospital to get Demerol shots, and on top of that he drinks excessively." The doctor was quite taken back, and to his credit he did phone the other doctors to let them know what was going on, and they did cut Dad off. I believe this action contributed to my dad getting clean and sober not long after this, and in fact, helped save his life.

One of the behaviors in my first marriage that distressed my wife the most was when I would go to the bar after finishing the day at college or work. Around 6 p.m., I would phone her from the noisiest part of the pub knowing she would recognize where I was. She would ask, "Where are you? You promised to come right home today." I would snap back, "Well, if you're going to be like that, then I'm not even going to come home," and I'd hang up the phone. I would set it up to be like that, purposely pushing her buttons so I could justify staying out and continuing to drink that night.

In some ways it was like fights I would get into, although I'm not a fighter. I'd be drunk and pick a fight with someone bigger and more capable, and most often get beaten up. Then I'd keep drinking. Man, if you had to go through what I went through, you'd keep drinking too! Such is the power of this disease.

The third "C" of an addiction diagnosis is consequences. Addicts continue to use and abuse drugs or alcohol despite significant negative consequences. Consequently, relationships will always deteriorate. Addicts consistently and increasingly abuse and hurt those they love the most, and who love them the most. As the drinking or using escalates and remorse and guilt set in, addicts start lying to these people—maybe telling half truths, but rarely full truths. So deception becomes a part of their daily living.

At the extreme end of the spectrum are the alcoholics or drug addicts who cannot begin to comprehend the serious consequences of their behavior: the cocaine addict who steals the purse of a helpless old lady; the mother on heroin who neglects her children for days; the alcoholic who ends up living on the street having lost his family, his home, and his job. It is hard to garner sympathy for these people, but the fact is, they no longer have the capacity to make rational decisions and set appropriate priorities and boundaries—the brain's ability to do this has been usurped by the addiction.

All ability to understand and appreciate concepts such as consequences is lost. Addicts, often when they stop using, have the knack of still *not* being able to look at the devastation they caused. They don't see the damage the tornado left in its wake. That is to say, they don't recognize the challenges and pain their behaviors inflicted on their relationships. When they do stop, they believe that everything is wonderful. It is almost as if they are seeking immediate gratification and acknowledgement, which makes sense since addicts crave attention. That is one reason why recovery is a long-term process, not just for addicts, but for their loved ones as well.

PATTERNS OF ADDICTION

It is a myth that people must drink or use excessively, or on a daily basis, to be considered addicts. Dean, a close friend of our family, for example, only drank a few times a year, but when he did, he'd go off on a bender that could last for a week or two. Dean was a farmer, and when he needed to take responsibility for the crops, he did so. But several times a year, in between responsibilities on the farm, he'd take off, to where no one knew, and drank to excess. Dean is an example of the most common pattern of addiction—going on benders—although in his case, the time between episodes was unusually long.

I too was a bender-type user. My pattern, like so many addicts, was to drink and do drugs on my days off work or school. It might look like this: during a regular work week, by about Tuesday or Wednesday, I'd start planning for a weekend of partying and drug use. By Thursday I might be having a few drinks in the evening. On Friday I'd head out straight from work or school and drink/use all weekend. I might not have even had the intention of carrying on all weekend, but that's how it usually worked out. By Sunday morning I'd be feeling so lousy and fed up I couldn't carry on. I knew I needed to be able to function the next day so I'd stop. Unless, of course, there was an activity later that day where I knew there would be alcohol or drugs, and I'd convince myself I could be there and not have to be concerned about any consequences.

As the illness progresses, bender-type addicts often start earlier in the week and frequently are not able to stop and straighten up enough to go back to work on time. They do what they have to in order to keep their employer or their partners off their backs. If they should lose their job, then there's nothing keeping them from using excessively on a daily basis.

Darlene, a young woman who recently celebrated her first year of recovery, is a good example of a bender-type addiction pattern. A mother of two young children, Darlene held down a responsible job for ten years. She'd frequently head out after work on a Friday and drink/use all weekend, not giving much thought to what was going on at home. This went on for several years until her partner decided he'd had enough. Two years ago, at his request, I got involved. Darlene did go to treatment and then relapsed on and off for a year. She knew that Friday nights were a trigger, so to help herself get through this particularly problematic time of the week, she started up a Friday evening 12-step recovery meeting with the support of other recovering addicts. She remains sober to this day.

Another pattern of addiction is where people drink or use drugs regularly, usually most days. You don't see them drunk or stoned because they know they need to be careful and are able to hold some parameters on their use. As described in the story of the apples at the beginning of this chapter, these people don't generally have just one drink. Once they have that first one, they have to have several. However, they have just enough control that you rarely see them intoxicated.

Professionals who need to ensure they keep up a certain image will work very hard to make sure they don't appear in public drunk or stoned. I've also known a number of homemakers who were heavy drinkers, but they'd have just enough control to maintain appearances. Again with this pattern of using, when you take away the parameters that work or family provides, the drinking/using inevitably takes off on them. For example, when the long-time worker finally retires or the homemaker's children leave home, the old parameters of responsibility are no longer there to keep them on 'the straight and narrow,' relatively speaking, and they succumb to the progression of the addiction.

As the disease progresses and the constraints are removed, addicts who go on benders and who drink/use fairly consistently will reach a stage where it becomes apparent to those in regular contact with them that these individuals are drug/alcohol dependent. They clearly meet the criteria of the three "C's" of addiction: they have little or no control over their using or drinking, they have an obsessive compulsion to drink/use, and they continue despite increasing negative consequences.

WHAT CAUSES A PROBLEM IS A PROBLEM

A question I am asked repeatedly is, "How do we know if someone who uses drugs or alcohol on a regular basis is in fact an addict?" We all know people who drink alcohol on a regular, consistent basis, or perhaps smoke marijuana daily, or abuse prescription drugs. Are these people addicts? Again, we need to look at the criteria of the three "C's," but ultimately, a diagnosis of addiction is best determined by an addiction professional.

In my travels throughout North America and abroad, I've encountered countless people who defend their drinking habits, explaining that while they enjoyed a few drinks most days, they remain in complete control of themselves and their drinking. They would become quite defensive saying that going to the local pub/drinking establishment, or having a bottle of wine with dinner most days was an activity shared by many cultures around the world—the French, Germans, Italians, British, Irish, etcetera—and there was nothing wrong with it. They claimed that they did not experience any negative consequences as a result of their drinking, and in fact, viewed their drinking as an enjoyable, social activity.

There is no denying that consuming alcohol on a regular basis is a part of the culture for many people in North America as well. A large percentage of the population enjoy a couple of beers or a glass of wine on a daily basis. There is generally nothing harmful with that. However, it is often the case that when people have one, they don't stop there but continue on to drink excessively time after time. This sustained pattern of drinking becomes a concern, certainly for their loved ones.

For me, the issue in this instance is not about being able to apply the label of addiction, but rather determining whether or not the drinking or using is causing problems for the individual or those who care about them. Father Martin, the addiction specialist I mentioned earlier, used to say: "***What causes problems is a problem. Correct it or the problems will worsen.***"

Inevitably, problems related to drinking and using show up in relationships, and are not always that obvious at first. Let's use an example of a husband and father who comes home from work and immediately pours a Scotch or opens a bottle of beer, and drinks it straight down, followed by another one or two or three. The wife may have been waiting for her husband to help her with some chores, or his daughter may have wanted her dad to play soccer with her at the park. But after just a few ounces of alcohol, he's too sapped of all energy and motivation to do much of anything for the rest of the evening. Instead, he opts to sit in front of the TV, not saying much to anyone. This pattern gets repeated frequently. This man would argue he is in control and making a conscious choice about his drinking, which is probably true, at least in the beginning.

In this example, however, the daughter grows up never really getting to know her father, never having developed a fun, loving relationship with him. Is this a problem? There's not been any obvious abuse of any kind, but in truth there has been—the girl feels neglected, dismissed, and perhaps to some extent, abandoned. Feeling neglected is a very common experience for children of addicts and substance abusers. It is possible the girl in this scenario, when she grows up, will feel unattractive, unworthy, and be emotionally needy in intimate relationships. When both parents drink or do drugs on a regular basis, the children suffer in so many subtle and not-so-subtle ways. Unfortunately we are seeing this more and more in our society today.

The wife also feels neglected and experiences an emotional impact just like the daughter, and it becomes a matter of time before she decides enough is enough, finds other activities to fill the void, and possibly ends up walking out. This man is probably unaware of the degree to which his drinking may be affecting the quality of his relationships with his wife and daughter. But what his behavior is saying is that having the drinks is in fact more important to him than being present and participating in the two most important relationships in his life.

This man would say that he enjoys a few drinks most evenings and it is simply a way to unwind at the end of a stressful day. But there is no doubt he is losing out too. Once he has a drink or two, activities with his family that he enjoys and may want to do, become too much of an effort. Bad feelings develop on both sides, everyone suffers, and problems persist. If this fellow continues to drink despite negative consequences, then a diagnosis of addiction is quite likely.

EMOTIONAL IMMATURITY

When associating with an addict it is important to appreciate that this is likely someone who is not as emotionally mature as his or her biological years would suggest. In many ways, addicts are unable to appropriately handle and express emotions. This is because their emotional growth was stalled or slowed down at the age at which they started drinking or using. It's a particularly frightening scenario when we think about young kids who start doing drugs as young as 10 or 12. At this early age, drug use completely thwarts their emotional development, and particularly affects the still-developing brain.

Of course, another reason for addicts' immaturity can be the fact that a high percentage of them come from homes with addiction where healthy relationships were not modeled, or they may have grown up in a similar scenario to that described in the last section.

It has been my experience that when addicts have quit using, maybe even for years, and they start drinking or using again, they quickly revert back to where they were at emotionally when they were using, or maybe even further back. The illness is awakened and all of the pain associated with drinking or using is forgotten, and they promptly return to the same way of thinking and acting, and to the same mental/emotional place they were in when using. This can happen even if people have worked on their emotional and personal growth during the years they abstained from drinking/using.

Many addicts suffer deeply rooted fear and anger issues that are usually linked to the past and have a lot to do with trust. Whether this is a higher proportion than the general population, I don't know. But I have observed that unresolved anger can fester beneath the surface for years and fuel the fire of addiction. If left unaddressed, it can be a major contributor to relapsing.

Underlying anger issues get lived out either aggressively, expressed by acts of verbal or physical violence, or passive aggressively, where it simmers inside as a silent resentment and often gets expressed as sarcasm and abrasive humor. In either case, their way of handling anger becomes a conditioned pattern of behavior that addicts believe is acceptable.

In the early months of their recovery, it is likely that much of the addict's accumulated anger and resentment will bubble to the surface and will need to be managed appropriately...or there will be a strong likelihood of relapse. There is a saying that anger is just one letter away from danger (d-anger), and this is very true for the addict in recovery.

A sign of immaturity I have noticed with many addicts is that they like to be rebels and intentionally go against the tide, just to be different or defiant. It is a classic case of addicts saying something is black when we say it's white. These people are generally quite proud of being rebels.

A few years ago a therapist pointed out to me that years of recovery will not equate with emotional maturity, unless the individual does the work that is described in the next few chapters. Recovery is the process of healing the parts of ourselves that were harmed because of the drinking or using that often began in our youth, or the parts of us that were torn apart or shredded during our upbringing.

THE ADDICT AND THEIR CONSCIENCE

What most addicts can't and won't see is the havoc they create for their family and home life. They expect (even demand) that somehow things will continue to be normal at home, while they are in fact creating the opposite environment. The absence of money or inappropriate spending of money, feelings of fear, shame, and embarrassment, cover-up and denial, all become an accepted part of family life.

But somewhere deep down inside, most addicts do have a conscience, a sense of right and wrong that gets triggered from time to time and which can contribute to erratic behavior. As their addiction progresses, addicts become increasingly more disappointed with themselves because they recognize they are not holding up their end of the deal and managing the responsibilities that are legitimately theirs, especially in their primary relationships.

There was a part of my dad that knew his family, particularly my mom, was paying a heavy price for his drinking. Throughout his drinking years, Dad almost always managed to hold down a job, but his money went, by and large, to drinking, gambling, and other women (these things tend to co-exist). It didn't mean he was prepared to stop, but he did try in his own peculiar way to make up for it.

Sometimes Dad would come home late after we were all asleep and if the dishes weren't done, or the floor wasn't swept, he would haul all four boys out of bed. He'd make us do the dishes or whatever it was he wanted done. It was so out of context. He would be angry, but not volatile. He would talk to us about the responsibilities we had at home, and that we shouldn't expect Mom to do it all. He would stay up with us until the work was done. Now what was that about? I believe he was angry at himself because of his absence of support for Mom and our home.

Other times, when we got up in the morning, there would be a huge colorful bouquet of flowers on the table. We'd know he'd been downtown drinking the night before, and must have driven home via the provincial parliament in Edmonton, where he would have stopped and *borrowed* some flowers from the beautifully manicured grounds of the legislature. If he'd been caught he'd probably have been thrown in jail. Again, what was it all about? Guilt and shame for sure, but also it was his attempt to show he cared, and make up for the pain and hardship he knew deep down that he caused my mom.

Fortunately, when we can work with an addict who has a conscience, we can increase the likelihood of success because he or she does know at some level what is happening. Most addicts do have a sense of right and wrong, and when you can combine that with an intervention process that is a mix of firmness and compassion, you can usually reach them, and be successful in helping them get on a path to recovery.

THE HIDDEN ADDICTION

I want to say something about a widespread problem that goes largely unnoticed in society—addiction to over-the-counter and prescription drugs.

Over-the-counter drugs can be bought anywhere by anyone, and large quantities can be purchased without questions being asked. Painkillers and cough mixtures that contain codeine and alcohol can be addictive with continued use and abuse. Teenagers will sometimes intentionally abuse over-the-counter drugs in order to experience a relatively inexpensive high.

As for prescription drugs, dependence often starts out innocently enough—painkillers needed to relieve pain after an accident—but the use continues long after the pain has subsided. Before long, the user feels he or she can no longer function without them. Unfortunately, the very doctors who prescribed the medications in the first place often don't recognize the signs of addiction.

With continued or excessive use of over-the-counter or prescription medications, problems will inevitably arise because some natural bodily function has been suppressed or hampered. For example, if something is taken which stimulates serotonin in the body, the body gradually loses its ability to produce serotonin without the stimulus of this drug. Long-term usage can eventually lead to liver and kidney damage, and even heart and blood pressure problems.

We often hear stories in the media about the very real dangers of taking legal drugs—mixing different prescription drugs has claimed the lives of many. Taking a drug in conjunction with alcohol can also be fatal. So can taking dosages larger than what was prescribed—my niece Patti died of an accidental overdose of liquid Demerol.

Unfortunately, addiction to a legal drug can sneak up on people without them or their family realizing it—as often happens with the elderly. When people stop taking prescription drugs, they suffer withdrawal and find it easier to go back on them, rather than dealing with the uncomfortable symptoms.

People who end up abusing legal drugs in so many ways are no different than people who abuse alcohol or illicit drugs. The same kind of behavioral patterns will develop, the same kinds of relationship problems will arise, and some type of treatment will be required for recovery.

CHAPTER THREE

&

OBTAINING RECOVERY

Whatever course you decide upon, there is always someone to tell you that you are wrong. There are always difficulties arising which tempt you to believe that your critics are right. To map out a course of action and follow it to an end requires...courage.

Ralph Waldo Emerson, 1803-1882, Poet and Essayist

That Saturday in February 1972 after I had what would be my last drink, I was desperate to do something—anything. The hit-and-run incident was the final straw that brought me to my knees, to the place where I was finally willing to reach out and ask for help. I had hit bottom and I knew I couldn't carry on with my life the way it was.

Hitting bottom is different for everyone. Most addicts aren't convinced that they truly are alcoholics or drug addicts in the first place. If they get to this stage, they just want to put an end to the problems of broken relationships, job troubles, loneliness, legal or financial issues, or whatever it is in their life that is wearing them down. They want to still have a drink, or maybe do drugs from time to time, but not have the incessant headaches and heartaches that go with their drinking or using.

The notion that someone has to have virtually lost everything before hitting bottom and being willing to reach out for help is a fallacy. Addiction is like an elevator that keeps going down and down. The elevator stops at different floors from time to time when something happens, and addicts can get off. Sometimes the right information at the right time is all that is required for them to see they have to make a change, get off the elevator, and take advantage of available help.

The family or the workplace can often help an addict get off the elevator at an earlier floor. Recovery literature talks about opportunities that "raise the bottom"—this could be a crisis or an intervention. Perhaps their job or marriage is on the line, or there has been some kind of legal trouble. However, if an addict chooses not to get off the elevator, it keeps going down and becomes much harder to get off.

My experience is that whether addicts decide to pursue recovery because someone else convinces them they should, or because they decide to seek help on their own, the chances of success are the same as long as they are willing to do the necessary personal work.

When I finally realized that I couldn't carry on living my life the way I had been, I knew from experience that I couldn't do it alone, and I had to reach out. Fortunately, I recalled the experience of my dad's buddy Bill who quit drinking a few years before with the support of recovering alcoholics. Bill and Dad worked and drank together for years, so when I heard that Bill had quit, it blew me away that he could do this and stay with it, while my dad continued to drink.

When I reached out in my time of need I was given the name of a person to call, which I did immediately. Dwayne, the person I called, was very supportive and accompanied me to my first meeting. I remember walking into that room feeling scared and unsure of what to expect, but within a short time the tremendous weight of my fears was lifted from my shoulders as an incredible sense of 'coming home' settled into my psyche.

After attending just a few meetings, I realized that I ought to listen to these people who had come before me. I just knew that if I wanted to change my life, I had to follow their advice and grow with it in depth and understanding.

THE PENNY DROPS

During the first few months, I still had not fully accepted that I was an addict. I knew intellectually that the difficulties in my life were tied to my using, I had tons of evidence around me to prove that was the case, but acknowledging and accepting one's addiction involves both the head and the heart. About the third month or so of recovery, I came home one evening after my recovery meeting and lay down on the bed in my black and red bedroom in the house I still lived in with my drinking and drug-using buddies. I thought about Sylvia and what I had lost, and for the first time I could honestly see the degree to which I was powerless over alcohol and drugs—that my desire to use had been stronger than my personal commitment to our marriage.

In that moment, the understanding of what I was dropped from my head into my heart. With it came a sense of freedom and release so strong that I felt like running down the street yelling "I'm an alcoholic, I'm an alcoholic." Again, I believe that reaching that point is different for everyone, and that it takes something very personal for the heart to open in this way. Now I understood with my whole being what I had been hearing at the meetings about powerlessness and the need for surrender.

In recovery programs, people are encouraged to stay involved. "Keep coming back. Keep coming back. It will rub off on you." There is also an expression that says, "Don't leave before the miracle happens." Reaching that point of whole-body understanding and acceptance that you are an addict is a two-part process. When you get it at the heart and soul level it is a miraculous, life-changing moment. I made the decision to go back and work on my marriage with Sylvia.

LESSONS FROM LEROY

Leroy, a businessman in his fifties with many years of recovery, acted as one of my first mentors, teaching me some of the most profound lessons for achieving sobriety. A good ol' red-necked Albertan, he didn't like social workers or governments, and he didn't believe in residential treatment. So along I came, a government social worker who was going off to residential treatment. I was everything he disliked. Nevertheless, he spent untold hours with me. I'd frequently call him at home quite late at night, but he always honored his commitment to be available if someone needed help.

He would say to me, "Before you pick up a drink or drug, phone me." Now that is an easy gesture to make, but when those in recovery say that, they mean it. So I would call him and he'd say, "Okay, I'm going to the shop out back to put on some coffee, the door is open." I'd drive over to his place, whatever the hour, and we'd talk for an hour or two. That kind of support made an enormous difference in the early years of my recovery.

As a professional in the addictions field, I strongly encourage clients to regularly attend recovery meetings. They provide a safe haven to learn the necessary steps in achieving and maintaining recovery, and they ensure that support and companionship are available to help avoid the deadly loneliness trap that all addicts are more than familiar with. But often, more support is needed outside the meetings, whether it's working with a professional counselor, attending residential treatment, or talking with an understanding friend. Leroy was always there for me. I didn't abuse that relationship, but I sure used it.

In our discussions, Leroy said to me, "If you plan to obtain and maintain any degree of continued, contented recovery, you will attempt to attend no less than two support meetings a week for the duration of your life that you plan on staying sober." ***Obtain, maintain, continued, contented, recovery***. Those five words were forever emblazoned in my consciousness. What do we have to do to obtain recovery? What do we have to do to maintain recovery? What do we have to do to have continued and contented recovery?

Leroy also taught me about the four daily responsibilities of recovery. I've never forgotten them, though there have been times when I did forget to practice them. He said to me, "Jim, when you get up each morning always remember, you are not a social drinker. Social drinkers are what we call 'normies' and you are not a normie."

He went on to say, "Normies have three daily responsibilities to guide them and keep life balanced, but you have four. Normies must first take responsibility for the health and well-being of their family, or if they live alone, for themselves. Second, they must be financially responsible by working hard at their job, or if they are not employed, they shouldn't sit around whining and complaining but get out and volunteer, and be in service to somebody. Finally, however it may fit, normies must be responsible for their social life because enjoyment in life is important. But since you are not a normie, you have a responsibility that comes before these three. That is to not drink or use any mood-altering drug that day."

He suggested that I put these four responsibilities on the fridge or bathroom mirror where I could read them every morning and review them at the end of each day.

He said, "If you willingly work these four responsibilities in this order, then you will stay on track. If you get them out of order for too long, it is only a matter of time before you fall back into some of your old ways of self-absorbed thinking. If it goes unaddressed you *will* eventually pick up that first drink."

Something that my first recovery group understood is that you have to have fun in recovery, a concept that was absolutely critical for me in those early days. One experience that stands out for me was a weekend retreat with the guys. Dwayne invited a group of us to a stag weekend at his family cottage to fish, play cards, and hang out. I thought this should be interesting. I'd never partied without booze or drugs, especially at a stag. In fact, I was sure that once we got there, the wine and beer would begin to flow, and maybe even some women would materialize out of thin air. Instead, it was a great weekend of clean fun and a real lesson for me that you don't need to be drinking or using to have an enjoyable time.

Over the years, I've participated in recovery groups that really appreciated this, so they would make it a priority to set up opportunities to get together that often included family and friends. I know of one group that had a baseball team in a community slow-pitch league with the name 'Canada Dry,' and the team's goal was to involve everyone who showed up to play.

Winning each game was not their objective. Instead, they were committed to full participation, joy, laughter, and camaraderie. The example they set was not only inspiring for other teams in the league, and for the spectators, it was a wonderful way to help the newcomer in recovery feel more comfortable. Because addicts have a tendency to be obsessive and highly competitive, here they got to learn that winning in life is all about full participation.

An incident in my early recovery that made a lasting impression on me was a fellow who kept coming to our meetings quite drunk, not obstinate, just drunk. I wondered how he would be treated, expecting the group might ask him to leave. Instead, he was treated with acceptance, compassion, and patience. The group consistently welcomed him to meetings, letting him speak, never putting him down. They understood his addiction and knew why he was coming.

Every week he would show up obviously inebriated. He would cry and talk about raising his kids on his own. People simply said, "He is not here by mistake. No one comes to recovery by mistake. We just need to be patient, patient, patient. This is between him and his Higher Power. You can carry the message, but you can't carry the body." This man eventually found full recovery and became the father he always wanted to be to his children. It was too late to save his marriage, but not too late for him to find himself.

It is my experience that recovery groups are the most open and accepting of any group I've ever known. It doesn't matter where you come from or what you believe, there is no judgment.

POWERLESSNESS AND SURRENDER

It took several months of going to support meetings before I really identified with the concepts of powerlessness and surrender. I believe that in order to obtain recovery, we first have to hit that place of realizing and accepting that our life, in most areas, is unmanageable, and that we are powerless over our addiction. Sure, some addicts have stopped by sheer willpower, but my experience is that within three months, people who do that are usually back using some kind of mood-altering drug (or activity) again, or they are living a miserable existence toughing it out.

Admitting we have no power over our addiction seems contrary to the belief that we are the creator of our own lives. I believe that there is a higher consciousness or energy, if you like, that we are a part of and that we can call upon to help us. Thus, we can choose to be co-creators with this Higher Power (or we can use the words God, Creator, Universe, etc.) in everything we do. When it comes to confronting the power of addiction, taking the position we are powerless and that our life is unmanageable is what allows us to get on the path of constructing the life which, deep in our hearts, we really want for ourselves.

Some people struggle with this notion of surrendering to a Higher Power. A friend of mine who facilitates recovery workshops talks about the self-delusions that stop addicts from entering into a life of joyful recovery. He says these must be overcome in order for addicts to reach a place where they can fully surrender and get out of their own way. These delusions are:

1. I am not an addict/alcoholic.

2. I am an addict/alcoholic but it's not my fault.

3. I am an addict/alcoholic, but there is little hope that I could ever change.

4. I am an addict/alcoholic, but there is no power greater than myself that will help me.

5. There is a Higher Power, but it is not more powerful than the power of alcohol, drugs, and addiction.

This is the cunning, baffling, and powerful side of addiction that preys on addicts' minds as they make every effort to quit and maintain recovery, especially in the early stages of recovery. It is the disease that creates the delusions in order to keep the addict from surrendering and finding recovery.

This notion of admitting our powerlessness is especially daunting for those who are otherwise professionally and financially very successful. Because they've had success managing other parts of their lives, and they are generally well-educated, they believe it's possible to control their drinking or using. I know of two successful stockbrokers, both alcoholics, who each died choking on their vomit. Both believed they were in control, but that false belief lead to their deaths.

Some people believe that they have to engage in a fight to conquer this problem. The addict is in one corner of the boxing ring and the alcohol or drugs are in the opposite corner. The addict punches and kicks and bangs this enemy, but the disease gets right back up and takes another licking out of the person.

Yet 12-step recovery literature states unequivocally that to conquer this disease, an addict must surrender. The winning strategy is to be able to face your opponent and say, "I don't want to fight with you. There is too much pain, too much sorrow, too much sweat and tears, and too much to lose. I surrender." When addicts symbolically step out of the ring, that act of surrender allows them to give up the battle... and eventually win the war. Winning the war may take numerous acts of surrender, working through the delusions, turning different situations over to a Higher Power, asking for help, and doing the work of recovery.

Some people associate admitting one is powerless with weakness, but it's not. It requires a strength from deep within to let go and surrender. When we are able to fully accept our situation, we can get in touch with a power higher than ourselves, and together with this Higher Power, we can make life manageable again.

Many people have a real difficulty with the notion of a Higher Power or God. In recovery circles, it is often said that G.O.D. can stand for a 'Group Of Drunks or Druggies,' or for the presence of 'Good Orderly Direction' or just add another 'o' and make it 'G.O.O.D.' Another couple I heard just recently are G.O.D. can stand for the 'Great Out Doors' or 'Grace on Demand.' If that is how some people want to accept a Higher Power into their lives, then I fully support them.

I find it so interesting that scientists who study addiction and brain functioning are now saying that addicts are in fact powerless over their compulsive behaviors. They also say that drugs will eventually commandeer circuits in the brain that are involved in controlling motivation. The good news is that anyone, with support from others, can take control and change the brain by adopting new beliefs and behavior patterns. So while some circuits of the brain are rewired because of alcohol and drug abuse, other circuits can be engaged to override those that have been hijacked.

A CLEANSING PROCESS

Most addicts believe their drug of choice is their best friend—it helps them avoid the negative feelings they prefer not to experience. Giving up their drug feels like abandoning an acquaintance of many years. That is why people new into recovery face two significant opposing fears that can be all-consuming, although they might not be able to articulate them until later. Some addicts fear that recovery *won't* work, that they won't be able to let go, especially if they have tried before and relapsed. Others are afraid that it *will* work, and they'll have to let go of their old friend and the lifestyle that goes along with the drinking and/or using. Addicts can actually have both fears going on for them at the same time.

There is another common fear for those in early recovery that is referred to as the "nameless fear," a form of anxiety or panic attack. These attacks can come very suddenly and without warning, but they don't usually last a long time if you just allow them to pass. I had this happen a few times.

I recall one attack coming over me that was so intense I wanted to pull the car over and rush to stand in the doorway of a large granite building. I figured that something solid and secure would keep me safe. It was irrational, but very real. I found that the longer I actively pursued my recovery, the less frequently I encountered these attacks.

Nameless fears can be a critical issue for people, especially in early recovery. They are the body's way of disposing of negativity, and are in fact part of the cleansing process. Another way the body (and the spirit) will do this is through dreams. Addicts in early recovery will frequently dream about using again. These dreams can be so real that when they wake up they aren't sure if they've used or not. I recall one such dream where I experienced such vivid feelings of guilt and shame that I woke in a panic, thinking about how I would admit my relapse to my recovery group, and that I now needed to change the anniversary date of my recovery. It took some time to figure out that I was still in bed and all was well. What a relief!

Dreams are a way for the body to rid itself of the internal pain and negativity that alcohol and drug abuse put us through—the body 'dreams it out.' The other purpose these dreams serve is to raise a flag that our subconscious wants us to draw closer into recovery right then. When I hear of this happening to people, I recommend they spend more time with their mentor, and increase their attendance at meetings in order to get support through this time. Their subconscious is speaking to them and it is better to be safe than sorry. It's extremely important for addicts in recovery to develop their intuitive skills, and learn to listen to what their body, mind, and spirit are saying.

In early recovery, all of these fears are good because they can be the motivation addicts need to stay away from temptation, and out of slippery places—places that can be triggers that result in relapse.

MESSAGE OF HOPE

Addiction is a highly complex illness, but it is treatable. I am a firm believer that recovery should ideally include an abstinence-based residential treatment program lasting several weeks. When I stopped drinking and using, I continued to go to work on my recovery while finishing the last few months of my three-year college program. In late June, I checked into a residential treatment center.

A good treatment program first and foremost helps addicts understand addiction is an illness that can be treated. The experience of participating in a therapeutic community also gives addicts the opportunity to do some deeper personal introspection. Treatment programs allow people to make connections back to where they got into difficulty, not just back to where they seriously started to abuse drugs. They are supported in going deeper into their family issues, and sorting out the problems and pain of their past. They learn it is not about blaming, or even about what is right or wrong, but about understanding the whole picture. Addicts come to understand that their family could only give away what had been given to them.

Treatment can also help people learn how to become full, productive members of society. Since most addicts have made such a mess of their relationships, they may need to learn normal social skills. Spending time in a residential treatment facility can give addicts an in-depth understanding of their addiction and their behaviors, and at the same time teach them some valuable life skills. It is said that treatment is about discovery, not recovery. In a therapeutic community we can begin the process of discovering who we are. Recovery happens when people leave treatment and actively work on a day-to-day basis at a program, not only of abstinence, but of personal and spiritual growth.

I attended a facility that took a multi-disciplinary, or biological/psychological/social/spiritual approach with the goal of total abstinence from all mood-altering drugs. The greatest value of such a program is its message of hope. Hope is such a critical element. Addicts have to believe that they can successfully develop a strategy for daily living, where it is not necessary to drink or use drugs. If we have surrender without hope, we have despair. But if we have surrender with hope, we have opportunity. Recovery truly is a personal journey that is all about hope. And there is *always* hope.

Going back to the scriptures, the word "hope" originally meant "absolute assurance." Today hope means a possibility, a likelihood that all will be well again. It is important to know that if people are willing to follow certain guidelines and practices and do the work of recovery, that there is absolute assurance they can successfully recover. They need to know they *can* have the life of their dreams, they *can* reconcile broken relationships and build new ones, and they *can* have a life and a career they love. When addicts are in the midst of their addiction, this can be near impossible for them to accept, but as they gain confidence in their recovery, their sense of hope increases.

Another value of a multi-disciplinary approach to recovery is the emphasis on a spiritual component. Addicts are most likely to be successful at long-term recovery if they follow a suggested and proven recovery process that supports them in building a solid spiritual base. This does not mean spiritual in terms of religion, although it may be that they choose to join or return to a church or faith. A spiritual foundation allows addicts to pursue recovery with greater ease and purpose, through a process of developing and nurturing their inner self.

GOING COLD TURKEY

When I'm working with clients now, the first thing I like to see is a complete medical evaluation with a physician who is an addiction medicine specialist. These specialists can make recommendations regarding treatment protocols and whether or not detoxification is required. This type of thorough assessment also establishes if there are any co-existing mental or medical issues that need to be treated. If you don't identify and treat all conditions, then attempts at recovery may well fail.

The first step of an abstinence-based treatment program is to stop using and rid the body of toxins that have accumulated from prolonged drug and alcohol use. But for someone who has been abusing alcohol or drugs for some time, stopping suddenly can prove to be extremely dangerous, as well as mentally and physically painful. In these cases, it is critical that addicts seek medically supervised detoxification, rather than trying to stop completely on their own.

The nature and severity of the withdrawal symptoms will vary considerably depending on the drug, and frequency of use. These days, however, few people use one drug exclusively so detoxification can be complicated. Most detox centers provide medical interventions to help diminish the potentially unsafe and uncomfortable symptoms of withdrawal from alcohol and drugs. Ideally, they also incorporate counseling and therapy to help with the psychological distress.

Without question, the drug from which withdrawal is the most difficult is alcohol. It can cause a variety of side-effects that include headaches, vomiting, sweating, restlessness, loss of appetite, and insomnia. More serious effects include delirium tremens (DT's) and seizures, which can be fatal. It is estimated that one in four alcoholic patients are at high risk of a withdrawal seizure if not medically treated during withdrawal.

Withdrawal from opiates, such as heroin and methadone, and many prescription drugs, also require medical supervision. However, other illegal drugs such as marijuana, crystal meth, and cocaine (crack) are easier to withdraw from and may not require a medical detox process. Detox centers use a variety of medications and procedures taking anywhere from three to 14 days.

Many residential treatment centers will not admit clients into their primary treatment program unless they have quit using for at least three to six days. Some private centers do have a detox capability, however, they often have limitations. For example, they're often not equipped to treat methadone withdrawal which requires specific protocols. Many addicts who need to detox usually end up going to a government-run detox center. Unfortunately, because there are not enough facilities, there is often a waiting period of up to a month to get in, which can be a huge deterrent for addicts who have finally made the decision to try to quit.

I worked with a long-term heroin user who decided, with some coaxing from his supervisor at work, to get clean. This client, I'll call him Paul, was not only using alcohol and morphine, but also methadone, supplied by a government clinic to help him cut back on his heroin use. It is quite common these days for people to use a combination of drugs like this. I called various detox centers but was told it would be several weeks before he could get in. Since he had made up his mind to quit, he attempted to stop on his own the weekend before his admission date for residential treatment. I escorted him to the treatment center, and while he claimed he had gone three days without using heroin, his drug test showed he had used methadone, and he was not allowed to stay.

A couple of weeks later, he attempted it again and managed to pass the drug screening, but soon found he was too ill to stay in residential care through a cold-turkey withdrawal. What Paul needed was a good two or three weeks, or even longer, on a graduated medically-supervised methadone withdrawal program, something most treatment centers aren't set up to do.

I have to say I get completely exasperated when trying to help those in situations like Paul's because there are so few detox facilities available. When someone finally reaches out for help, immediate action and support is needed, or else the opportunity can be lost for good.

A DRUG IS A DRUG IS A DRUG

I've met many people who have quit one mood-altering drug because they realized they were addicted, but thought it would be okay to continue using another substance. They'll say, "I don't need to worry about marijuana, it is just alcohol that's a problem." Another might say, "I don't need to quit drinking, I just need to stop using narcotics because they cause trouble for me." I am a solid believer that whatever you call it, a drug is a drug is a drug. Anything that is mood-altering for addicts will eventually become a drug of choice and dependence because it is the altered mood they crave.

Again, research is finding that drugs, alcohol, and tobacco all impact the same region of the brain. All of these drugs masquerade as natural chemicals by affecting the brain's reward circuits. The most addictive drugs work either directly (cocaine and amphetamine), or indirectly (nicotine and alcohol). Opiates cause the release of dopamine, the chemical that triggers our pleasurable experiences. Any addict who thinks one drug can be substituted for another, and not become addicted, is sadly mistaken. That part of the brain where addiction lives cannot discern what drug is being used, nor does it moralize. People do.

Overcoming addiction involves much more than just fighting the compulsion to use. People think that if only there was a pill that took away the craving, then all would be well. While there are medications available that will mask the craving for certain drugs, that doesn't mean an addict is cured. Sometimes those medications are necessary in the short-term to stabilize the client, yet some of them are more addictive than the drugs they're designed to mask the craving for. Scientists are now telling us that to overcome addiction, we need to change our thinking and our behaviors, so that we, in fact, rewire our brains. That takes time and a lot of effort.

I'm very encouraged about some of the new medical research that is going on in the addiction treatment field. Scientists are looking to specifically treat the brain's mood regulatory systems that have been damaged by substance abuse and perhaps weakened by genetic factors from birth. They are finding that in addition to taking a 12-step facilitation approach, the use of genetic testing, diet, food supplementation, and exercise can significantly aid in the recovery process. I believe the future holds great promise for the successful treatment of addiction.

DAD, MY BROTHERS, AND RECOVERY

Eight months into my recovery, I decided it was my duty to get my father sober. By then I felt as though I had the equivalent of a Ph.D. in addictions. At this stage of his addiction, with bottles hidden throughout the house and garage, Dad not only drank vodka and beer whenever he could, he also had three separate doctors prescribing different drugs.

When Dad finally agreed to go to his first meeting with me, I stopped by the mechanic shop where he was working to pick him up. I was keyed up with excitement and anticipation that Dad would finally start dealing with his addiction issues, and he and I might regularly attend meetings together. As we stood in front of the shop talking, one of Dad's workmates pulled up in his Buick convertible with the top down. There, sitting on the rear seat in clear view, was a bottle of Lamb's Old Navy Rum, one of Dad's favorites. We spotted the bottle at the same time and my heart stopped beating. I locked onto his eyes knowing he didn't have the ability to make the choice to leave, for I knew that feeling. Sure enough, when I asked if he was ready to go he declared, "No, son, I'm going to stay here."

That was when I consciously 'let go and let God.' I knew this was not between Dad and me, but between my dad's conscience and his

Higher Power. I went on my own feeling deflated, but then I remembered something that Leroy had said to me. "Jim, your father has the right to drink, even if it is to oblivion or death. If it was simply black and white, you would just need to hit him over the head with a two-by-four." I realized years later that Leroy was talking about what the recovery community calls detachment, the need to let go and separate ourselves from the adverse effects that another person's addiction can have upon our lives. When we detach, we can begin to make more sense of our reality.

With detachment comes the realization that no situation is really hopeless, and that it is possible for us to find contentment, and even happiness for ourselves, whether the addict is using or not. There is a deep sense of relief when we come to see that we have the right to release and let go of our fears about the addict's using. When we detach from an addict, it doesn't mean we give up hope or abandon the person. There is always hope, even for the late-stage addict—but it will take a lot of patience, compassion, and determination.

When I truly succeeded in letting go of the need to 'fix' Dad, I was able to focus on my own life, going deeper into the process of recovery. The lesson I learned attempting to help Dad can be summed up in one statement: *The more you love, the closer you are, the more you see, the more it hurts, the less capable you are of directly changing that person—love them, learn about the addiction, and get out of the way!* I often use this when talking with groups about addiction.

My dad did start going to meetings not long after this incident and he participated in a residential treatment program near the end of

1972. He relapsed not long after getting out, and for my mom, that was it, she moved out. In less than a month of her leaving, Dad quit for good at the age of 58. We spent a lot of time working on our recovery together. I was so proud of him. It took him almost a year of just absorbing everything before he felt comfortable enough to share his story at our recovery group.

Three years into his recovery, Dad asked Mom, his true love, to remarry him. He and Mom went on their second honeymoon where Dad suffered a massive heart attack and died. Years of drinking, popping pills, and smoking cut his life short, but he passed from this world leaving the most beautiful legacy for his family that any alcoholic or drug addict could—he left as an active member in recovery. With 36 months of recovery he put a beautiful cover on his book of life. Our family was both proud and grateful that he was able to do that.

Not long after Dad sobered up, my oldest brother Darrel dropped by the house one evening wanting to have a heart-to-heart talk with me. He'd been drinking, but wasn't drunk. Darrel was a father of four children and his marriage was in difficulty. His anguish was obvious, so I candidly asked him how he felt about his life. I asked: "If your life were to end this very day, would you leave feeling proud of the person you have become, of how you treat yourself, your family, your job? Do you have a true sense of self-worth, self-respect, pride or personal integrity left?" He answered no to each of them.

I remember putting my hand on my heart and asking, "Darrel, tell me what more than our ability to breathe can be taken from us? Because of our drinking and our lifestyle, we've lost so much. I'm starting my life over again, and you can too. Before I move to Vancouver next week, I'd love it if you would join Dad and myself at our recovery group." Darrel did go to a meeting with us, and to this day, he has never had a drink, despite many challenging times, including the death of his daughter Patti at age 41 from an overdose of Demerol.

My brother Doug took me by surprise a few years later when he called and asked to meet privately with me. He shared that he too had recently quit drinking. It was a shock because I had never seen him drunk. He confided that he drank to excess mostly when he was alone at home. It was not unusual for him to end up crawling from the bathroom to the bedroom, too drunk to stand. He made the decision on his own to quit. He also quit smoking at the same time as he knew for him they went hand-in-hand and he had to quit both. Doug is one of those rare people who can quit successfully with just the support of friends and family. Although he doesn't go on his own, Doug will come along when there is a celebration of recovery for one of his family.

CHAPTER FOUR

ॐ

INTERVENTIONS

"How poor are they that have not patience. What wound did ever heal but by degree?

William Shakespeare, 1564-1616, Poet and Playwright

Helping someone get started on the road of recovery requires considerable patience and understanding. Kevin's story is a good example. The son of a senior executive of the company I worked for, Kevin had a love affair with cocaine such as I had not seen before nor since. He might have been a professional hockey player, but sometime in his teens he needed to feel accepted and make a statement, and in the process he was seduced by drugs.

When his parents came to see me, Kevin was 18 and living at home, doing all the things addicts do: lying, manipulating, and stealing. As the situation progressively worsened, I counseled them to ask him to move out, then change the locks on their house and put in a security system. I met with them regularly and had them attend Al-Anon and Tough Love meetings. I coached them that under no circumstances were they to give money to Kevin. They might buy him a meal now and again, but they were never to give him the means to buy drugs. I tried to get together with Kevin regularly as well, but he would show up only occasionally on the street corner where we arranged to meet.

Things went from bad to worse over the next year or so as his addiction deepened. Weighing just over 90 pounds, with needle marks scaring his arms, he ended up living in Vancouver's skid row district. His parents would climb several creaky flights of stairs in the dilapidated old hotel where he lived, to visit with him and let him know they loved him and had not forgotten him. Because Kevin was their only child together, their love was so deep and their hope so intense, they did everything they could under the circumstances to support him. This, of course, often just fed into his manipulative ways and kept his life going in a downward spiral.

Finally, I had to ask his parents, "Can you see in your heart that this boy is in the process of dying? Can you see that what you are doing in the name of helping him is contributing to his death?" I asked them to close their eyes and visualize his funeral, and to think about what they would want to say to him at the end. As morbid as that sounds, I had to jolt them enough to stop their over-protective behaviors. Only then might they be able to let go enough so that Kevin would no longer be able to manipulate them.

Again, I encouraged them to show their love by being there, taking him out for dinner, even taking him home for a meal. But if they did take him home, they needed to ask him not to lock the bathroom door, and they were to stand by the door until he came out. At the end of the evening, they were to take him back downtown and drop him off, even though everything in their being would want to hang onto him and keep him sheltered and safe.

Over the next year, various people got him into detox and he did a six-week residential treatment program. Unfortunately, not long after he got out he started using again. We all continued to hang in there for him. I always held out hope for him because I knew about his upbringing, and that he had a conscience deep inside we could work with.

At one point Kevin told us he needed $400 to pay off his dealer before the dealer came after him. His dad agreed to loan him the money. I told Kevin I'd take him, but the deal was that he was not there to buy. Some time later he admitted to me he didn't owe the dealer, he went there to score some cocaine.

People might say we shouldn't have trusted him, but sometimes you have to work an addict forward one issue at a time. We needed to show him we were prepared to trust him so that he would trust us. I made sure to tell him, "If you're lying it won't hurt me or your family, and the $400 is no big deal to your dad. If you are going to buy drugs, I am not going to know that, but you will, and it will eat at you. It is your addiction that is lying." He went in like it was his mission to pay off his debt, and came out proudly looking like he'd completed it, but it was all a lie.

I often talk about the need to be reasonable, respectful, and fair in life's dealings. We could have used an emotional sledgehammer and told him we didn't care if the dealers came after him. I think if we'd been talking about thousands of dollars it might have been a different matter, but in this case it was reasonable. Was it respectful? I don't respect dealers, but I do respect debt—that if you owe it, you pay it. Was it fair? Sure. Kevin was called to put his cards on the table. We wanted to be fair and give him the same chance to deal fairly with us.

You can take addicts to the next step and then another step further in this way. If you treat an addict with love and compassion, but with strength and firmness at the same time, you can make progress. Kevin knew he was lying. We could see at the time that his conscience was beginning to get the better of him.

Not long after this episode, Kevin, still in difficulty with his addiction, once again reached out for help. I made arrangements to have him admitted to a hospital detox in the interior of BC. This was followed by residential treatment, and then supportive living, which took a total of three months. He then participated in a six-month life skills training program before going on to post-secondary education. All this time he was very active in a recovery program for drug addicts. Kevin did everything he needed to do to obtain and maintain continued recovery. He went on to get married, have a couple of children, and earn a Master's degree. He now works as a counselor at a treatment centre.

Looking back, working with Kevin was such a blessing for me. The celebration ceremony for his first year of recovery was one of the most moving recovery celebrations I have ever attended. God's presence was very tangible in that room. With each person with whom I work, there are new insights for me. Being able to help someone turn their life around is personally very rewarding. Truly though, the greatest gift I've ever received in my life is to have moved through addiction and recovery myself, so that I can use my experience, strength, and faith to touch the lives of others. It humbles me to think I was chosen to do this work.

GETTING ON THE SAME TEAM

There are many different ways to confront someone who is abusing drugs or alcohol, and to help them get onto a path of recovery. I imagine what comes to mind for most people when you say the word intervention is the kind you see on reality television shows, what might be called a 'formal' intervention. This is a tried and true way to go in many cases, but it is not generally how I approach most interventions I undertake.

One formal intervention I did do was for the brother of a work colleague. In our discussions, my friend shared how deeply concerned he and his family were about his brother, a powerful and successful American businessman whose drinking had gotten way out of control. I asked to meet with the immediate family members to discuss his drinking history and their hopes for the situation, and I began to determine the willingness, emotional strength, and capability of each member to participate in a formal intervention process.

Preparing for the intervention is a process of two to four meetings with family members, possibly appropriate close friends, and often one or two professional, business or work associates. Each such intervention follows some core principles, but each one is as unique as the families seeking help for their loved ones.

In this particular case, all the family members made a list of every time this man's drinking had been a concern for them, starting back as far as they could remember, and bringing the list right up to date. They were to be as specific as possible, recording what had happened, when it happened, where it had happened, who was present at the time, and how it made them feel (we were after the feelings here). It didn't matter if other family members recorded the same events, as each person would have a somewhat different emotional response to the same situation.

We met again, each person went through their list, and we worked on them together. We rehearsed it and then made plans to do it for real. Everyone was understandably nervous when the time came.

When you do these intervention meetings, you have to screen out anybody who emotionally won't be able to deal with it—tears are okay, but not anger. In this case, we had worked through all that. Everyone was prepared, participants had been instructed not to engage in any dialogue with him, even if he tried to do so.

I still remember the horrified look on this fellow's face when he walked into the room and we told him why we were all there. He looked like he was going to bolt, but I did my best to put him at ease, careful not to oversell what we were doing. I asked him to be open and willing to listen as each person present shared his or her list.

The key to reaching addicts is to be able to touch their hearts in a warm and compassionate way, at the same time that you are requesting something of them. The challenge with most people, whether they are family members, friends, or co-workers, is that they generally don't have any knowledge or understanding of this disease, and so they become controlled by the addict's behaviors and emotions. They feel like they are constantly walking on thin ice and living in a reactive mode.

Most people who live with or spend time with an addict end up just putting up with frustration after frustration, while inside their feelings are building up until they finally erupt and unload their anger and fury at the addict. Sometimes, this scenario simply plays into what addicts want. This kind of outburst justifies for addicts why they drink or use in the first place, "This is nuts—I'm getting out of here," and off they go. People will often put up with the addict deciding to say nothing and then they end up blowing up.

I like to use the analogy of a baseball game to explain the dynamics that can go on for some families. Normally the catcher controls the game by calling the plays. But the addict playing in the outfield takes control and starts telling the other players what to do. The other players want to do something to change the game, but don't know what they can do on their own, so each one just gets more and more frustrated. It is critical for the addict never to allow the team to go to the dugout at the same time where they might start talking and figure out a way to wrestle power away from him. The addict is terrified of this, which is exactly why during an intervention, the goal is to get everyone on the same team, playing by the same rules.

In the case of this family, each member was to start by expressing their love or admiration and then say, "but here is how your drinking has affected me, and here is my request of you." The hope is that each person will touch the heart of the addict. When you can demonstrate with compassion how the addict's behavior is destroying each person in the family, in most cases, he or she will agree to go to treatment.

This man was so moved by the intervention that he willingly agreed to go to treatment at one of the finest facilities in the U.S. However, shortly after he got out, he relapsed. Now, I always hope a relapse doesn't happen, but I don't personally consider relapse to be a failure in the early stages because addicts will then see that this is a disease and they don't own it…it owns them. There is the possibility that relapse could be a step toward death, but frequently it is the path to acceptance that this is truly a disease, not merely a habit that can be controlled. With every relapse there will be an outcome. The outcome for this man was a car accident where he nearly lost his life. He went to treatment for a second time and has carried on successfully from there.

These formal interventions essentially hold up a mirror to the addict. That is why when you see these done on television, as in real life, the person frequently breaks down emotionally. It can be extremely moving for everyone, particularly the addict who finally drops the veil of denial.

I undertook a formal family intervention where I knew everyone involved quite well. The family was well prepared, but 10 minutes into it, the addict left the house and took off in his car. This man was a successful self-employed businessman who was not used to answering to anyone. People like this can be the most difficult of all to work with and I had warned the family he may resist. Nevertheless, the family was horrified that he walked out and they were deeply afraid he would be furious with them. A couple of weeks later, however, he called me wanting to talk. This man did go to treatment and got on a path of recovery, but in the end his marriage did not survive. Addiction will test any relationship, and often relationships are the first to go because the addict is so self-absorbed.

An interesting outcome of this case was that one of the man's sons who participated in the intervention ended up going to residential treatment himself, even before his dad went. Every intervention is different, and there is no way of knowing how each will turn out.

WORKPLACE INTERVENTIONS

For 26 years I worked for a Canadian multi-national corporation of 24,000 employees as Director of the Employee and Family Assistance Program. Managers across the country, and sometimes around the world, would call upon me to intercede with an employee suspected of having an addiction problem. When I undertook corporate interventions at the request of management or union leaders, the process frequently needed to be quite different from those done on my own time.

To illustrate, I worked with a Human Resources manager, I'll call him Tom, who came to see me at the request of his boss. Tom talked openly with me about his drinking, his wife's drinking, the fact that people in the company were obviously concerned about him, and that he knew his life was not working the way he wished it to. Nevertheless, he wasn't sure he or his wife were alcoholics or needed to go for treatment. I asked him to describe his level of personal satisfaction over his decision-making ability as it related to his drinking. He replied, "Not very good." I responded, "What you are telling me is that some of your finest thinking has got you to this place."

After a few sessions I asked him, "Would you be willing to trust me, given that I have some expertise in these matters, and let me make a couple of decisions for you?" I could see his body tighten up at this, but nevertheless he said he'd think about it. When he came back a few days later he assured me he was willing to do what I asked of him.

I told him, "I'd like you and your wife to meet my buddy Bob. He has been where you are at now, and I'd like you to follow through on whatever he recommends." Bob was a businessman who had a number of years of sobriety. He convinced Tom and his wife to begin attending recovery meetings.

Even though they went regularly for several weeks, they continued to drink. One night after a meeting Tom finished a glass of wine and then announced to his wife that was it, he would not drink again. His wife then finished off the bottle and she too said that was it. Neither one ever drank alcohol again. Tom would laugh and tease her that he had more time in recovery than she did, but only by an hour.

With his recovery, Tom began to enjoy life to the fullest and he paved the way for many people to get on the road of recovery. His transformation allowed him to reconcile with one of his daughters who had not spoken to him for 12 years. Tom and his wife became dear friends and an inspiration to me and many others. They were both very active in doing the work of recovery, being of service to others, and attending their support meetings.

Tom and his wife attained sobriety without going to residential treatment. While I am a strong believer in the value of residential treatment, I also recognize that not everyone needs to go this route to achieve contented recovery. I know many people who have done very well through regular attendance in recovery fellowships, others through committing whole-heartedly to their faith, and still others through participating in personal therapy, or some combination thereof.

Another example of a corporate intervention involved a senior officer. The president of the company asked me to help him with this man who had been seen in public embarrassingly drunk. I suggested we invite him—we'll call him Larry—to meet privately with the president and me in the president's office. This was our initial attempt to direct Larry towards acknowledging his drinking problem and agreeing to go for residential treatment.

I told the president that Larry would most likely argue that his drinking was not a serious problem, and that residential care or other treatment wasn't necessary. Larry would tell us that he could control his drinking from now on and that there would be no more episodes or concerns. I explained that it was at that moment that we should 'cast the net,' asking that if, in the future, there was another concern with his drinking, he would agree to do all that was requested of him. Larry's ego, as would be the case for most addicts, placed him in the position of setting his own trap for a future catch. Usually within six months, the addict gets caught in the net he or she so confidently agreed to.

As expected, Larry assured us that there was nothing to be concerned about because he was in control and that he would comply with all our recommendations if another incident occurred. Within a matter of months Larry got into difficulty again, but the net was cast. We reminded him of our agreement and he obligingly went off to residential treatment in the U.S. I met with his wife and family while he was gone in order to counsel them.

A couple of weeks into his treatment, the center phoned to tell us that Larry had tried to convince the staff he didn't have a problem, that this whole thing wasn't serious and he definitely didn't have any issues at work. The next day, rather than just phoning, I flew down with another senior officer of the company to meet Larry and give him a letter from the company president. We met Larry and his counselor to tell them that we were there to support Larry, but that clearly he was indeed in serious difficulty at work. If he did not successfully complete residential treatment and meet the conditions of a two-year continuing-care agreement, he would be let go from the company.

Larry's family had also communicated the gravity of their concerns. All of this combined ensured that he understood what was at stake. Larry got sober, but did relapse for a brief time early in his retirement. Fortunately he managed to get back on track with his recovery and remain there.

FAMILY FIRST

When my colleagues and I do workplace training on the single most commonly asked question is: "How do you help someone you suspect or know has a problem, when that person is unwilling to recognize it or deal with it?" In the majority of cases, they are asking about a family member or close friend, not about a coworker.

My response is the same as what I learned from my experience with my father: *The more you care, the closer you are, the more you see, the more it hurts, the less capable you are of changing that person—care about them, learn about the addiction, and get out of the way!*

Family members and loved ones should become educated about addiction and get as informed as they possibly can. Then they need to get out of the way and seek professional help.

When my stepfather had a stroke, my family, including Mom and me, went to the Heart and Stroke Foundation to learn all we could about what was happening to him. It took several sessions, reading the materials provided, and talking with others who had family members suffering from strokes, to establish a basic understanding of the types of strokes, the severity, and the most likely short- and long-term outcomes. Even with this understanding, Mom eventually had to see a therapist in order to know how to handle my stepfather's emotional stroke-related outbursts, and how not to take them personally.

Many people grow up with, or as adults live with, a substance dependent family member. Yet they have never spent any time getting educated to understand how their actions can perpetuate this devastating illness.

In almost all interventions, my focus is on the family first. When the family is engaged and educated, those behaviors that are actually supporting the addict can be significantly reduced. Then there is a much greater chance for success when it comes time to deal with the addict's continued use. There are several ways for family members to become educated: get one-on-one counseling with a therapist who understands addiction as an illness and its impact on families; attend meetings of a 12-step program for loved ones of addicts or an open meeting of a recovery program; attend a family program at a residential treatment center; and read about the illness (there is considerable information online). My preference is that they do all of the above. When family members are educated about drug addiction and the role they can play, the likelihood increases considerably that they and their loved ones will get the help they all need.

If family members are able to participate in a week-long family program at the same facility the addict attends, either at the same time or later, another level of learning and understanding takes place. Family members develop a common language and bond, and with an understanding of how the disease has affected their family dynamics and impacted individual family members, a complete healing is possible.

A condition I set before agreeing to work with families who want help is that they be willing to do all that I ask of them. If they have an issue, or if they are going to waver, they have to talk to me. Sometimes I end up working with families for weeks, even months, before we approach the addict. A family must be prepared to deal with the state of denial and defensiveness in which an addict lives. Frequently adult family members have grown up in homes where a parent was an addict, so it is not just this situation—it is a whole lifetime of relationships where they've lived in the realm of addiction and denial.

Often in the later stages of the disease, family members are worse off emotionally than the addict. Addicts have the advantage of going through the turmoil they create, numbed by the alcohol or drugs they use. But loved ones, unless they are doing drugs themselves, have to deal with all of the raw emotion on their own. It's no surprise that family members always have their own healing to complete. It is desirable that this begins to happen *before* we move forward with the addict.

When families go to regular support meetings or a treatment program, I counsel them that it is not always necessary to tell the addict what they are up to. Addicts are exceedingly sensitive and believe that everybody is talking about them and treating them as if they are different. In their minds they find this all very condescending. If a family member were to say, "I just love you so much and I want to do this to help you," the addict would feel patronized. I tell family members that if the powerful intuitive abilities of the addict do pick up on something, they should be honest and share what they are doing and why. Otherwise, they should just go to the meetings and programs and not make a big deal of it. When family members take care of themselves first, it is a very different psychological motivator for the addict. If the addict expresses interest in what the family members are doing, I tell them to give the addict my business card and have them call me when he or she wants to talk.

I have come to expect the unexpected when doing interventions with families. A woman asked me to do an intervention with her cocaine-addicted husband, and so we undertook somewhat of a formal intervention with the participation of the wife, the man's best friend, his nephew, and several others. This fellow was not willing to go to residential treatment, but he agreed to attend recovery meetings, which he did. But, while he claimed to have quit, he was in fact using every couple of days. In the meantime, his wife, his best friend, and his nephew all came to me with substance use issues of their own. The wife and the best friend attended a six-day family program at a residential treatment center. The wife then got involved in a recovery group for herself, and the friend went back to attend the primary residential treatment program. The nephew also began going to recovery meetings.

Three of the participants in the intervention ended up in recovery, and the cocaine addict continued to use. Just over two years have now passed. The marriage ended, the wife received her second-year recognition in recovery, as did the friend. The nephew experienced a few brief relapses, but is now a few months away from celebrating his second year of recovery.

CHAPTER FIVE

ഇ

RELAPSING

Our greatest glory is not in never falling, but in rising every time we fall.

Confucius, 557 BC - 479 BC, Chinese Philosopher

The pastor from my mother's church phoned me the morning of February 24, 1996 to tell me my sister Cheri had passed away from what appeared to be a heart attack. She was 44 and had been suffering from systemic lupus for 15 years. My whole family was stunned when the results of the autopsy came in a couple of days later. Cheri had died of a heart attack brought on by a cocaine overdose. She had been clean and sober for years... or so we thought.

As the two youngest in the family, Cheri and I grew up with the worst of Dad's alcoholism. When we were in our late teens and early twenties, we would often party together. She was addicted to several drugs, especially to marijuana, smoking it first thing in the morning and throughout the day whenever she could. As she struggled at different times for recovery, it was no surprise she relapsed to using marijuana first as her drug of choice. Despite what some people try to claim, marijuana is a dangerous drug and it can be very addictive, especially given today's potency levels.

Cheri's story of multiple relapses is not unusual. Like many addicts she worked hard at recovery going for residential treatment at least three times. She even helped establish a treatment center for First Nations people on Vancouver Island. My impression was that her relapses were generally related to her personal relationships. It was no surprise that Cheri attracted a series of relationships with men who were emotionally and/or physically abusive and who were addicts themselves. Her wounds tended to attract other wounded souls who needed healing. We came to see her relapses as part of her disease in her ongoing journey, and the best we could do was to love her and pray for her.

Despite her arduous life, she was a very loving, engaging, and accepting human being. She had a wonderful connection with First Nations people. Both her children have First Nations ancestry, her daughter Ashley from the Bella Coola band and her son Calvin from the Alert Bay band. Her funeral was a beautiful blend of a Christian and traditional native service where we all celebrated the life and death of this beautiful, but anguished soul.

Cheri's death was a huge loss for her two children and for the rest of the family. It was especially hard on my mom because she and Cheri talked every night. Mom lost her only daughter, her youngest child, and her best friend.

SLIPPERY SLOPES

Many addicts relapse because they believe that after a period of being clean and sober they can handle moderate alcohol or drug use. Instead they end up getting hooked all over again, never managing to get back to sobriety.

One such example is the story of Guy, a fellow I met in the early days of my recovery. Guy owned and operated a service station just outside of town. When he celebrated three years of sobriety at the age of 35, I recall being awe-struck that someone that young could go so long without a drink. Just before he was to celebrate four years of sobriety, Guy relapsed. In a matter of only one year he lost everything, his marriage, his house, the business. When I heard what happened, it hit me hard.

Then there was Ted, another young guy I met in my first year of recovery. He'd been a chronic alcoholic for a number of years. Unemployed, he'd been sober for just a few months. He came to a meeting one night and told us he'd been offered a job working for a liquor distribution company, and wanted to know what others thought. One of the fellows replied, "You gotta do what you gotta do, but it is probably too early for you yet to step into such a slippery place. You might want to wait until you are sober at least a year." Well, Ted thought he knew better as most addicts do. He accepted the job and we didn't see him for a few months. Then one day we heard that he had taken his life with a rifle in the basement of his house. Sadly, he only lived a few blocks away from where we held our recovery meetings.

Another fellow I knew relapsed after 16 years of active recovery. He sold his business pocketing more than a million dollars, and for whatever reason, he started drinking again. One night he showed up at our recovery meeting clearly under the influence and said to the group, "I want you guys to know that everything is okay. I can handle my drinking now. I made a good business deal and I'm doing okay." Within a year, he had lost his marriage, his home, and died of alcohol-related health complications.

RELAPSE CUES

As mentioned earlier, I always hope people stay clean and sober from the start, but if they do relapse in early recovery, I don't see it as a failure. The illness tricks people into believing they can manage drinking or drug-use. Their justification: "It's just a drink now and then, or a couple of tokes after all, and I'm doing some personal work, so now I should be able to control it." In a very short time, they are right back where they left off. Hopefully that first relapse scares the hell out of them.

A fear of relapsing again can be beneficial because now the addict should have absolute confirmation that this is a disease that is beyond his or her control. Once a person has that first drink or drug, whatever it is, the choice is taken away from them. It is not the tenth drink or toke that gets addicts into trouble…it is the first one. There's a saying in recovery that if you don't take the first drink, you will never break out into a drunk—guaranteed! In recovery literature, this is referred to as the phenomenon of craving and it is unique to addicts.

Brain researchers tell us that avoiding that first drink or drug use can be a challenge for the recovering addict because environmental or emotional cues can trigger the brain circuitry to generate a powerful craving. Once that craving kicks in, the likelihood of a relapse is strong. As soon as addicts ingest the drug, any control quickly vanishes and they will likely keep abusing…and the cycle continues with crisis after crisis.

This kind of craving is a physical phenomenon that stops once the substances are removed from the body, but the obsession in the mind doesn't quit. The power of the mind is such that it tricks people into believing they can handle their drug of choice and one more time won't hurt.

Environmental cues that act as triggers can be other individuals, physical or emotional places, and activities. Scientific studies have confirmed what many in the field have long known, that there is an emotional memory associated with using a drug that includes the whole environmental context of what was happening at the time an addict was using—the places he or she frequented, the paraphernalia, the rituals, the people. Through classical conditioning, all of this is attached to the drug-using experience and any one cue can be enough to trigger a craving. When I quit drinking, people I knew with many years of recovery asked me what my favorite drink had been, and I said rye whiskey and

Coke. They advised that I not drink Coke for a year or two because it could trigger a craving for whiskey.

To caution people about emotional cues, recovery programs often use the acronym H.A.L.T. as a guidepost. They say, "Don't let your body/mind/spirit get too Hungry, too Angry, too Lonely, or too Tired." Any combination of these could trigger cravings and potential relapse.

The most insidious of these states for people in recovery is loneliness. When I was using, I'd go to parties and appear to be having a great time, but inside I was desperately lonely. Loneliness is quite different from being alone. It is a deep sense of feeling empty inside. In response to feeling this way, the addict makes desperate attempts to fill the void with external activities and possessions.

Addicts aren't particularly good at building and maintaining meaningful long-term, in-depth relationships, especially intimate love relationships. They often bounce from relationship to relationship, or maybe maintain one for a time, but then operate outside of it, which then affects their honesty and integrity.

Another pervasive emotional cue is resentment. Addicts are very selfish, self-centered people and it takes a long while to work through this. In early recovery, addicts have feelings of resentment about many things that are going on in their life—past, present, and future. Many of these people have lost their primary relationships, but have not emotionally dealt with the loss. Recovery programs often state that "justified resentments" are a luxury that addicts can't afford. I've heard it said that resentments are like alley cats—when you quit feeding them, they go away.

If people get to the point where they are on the verge of relapsing, before they pick up that first drink or drug, I recommend that they look straight at it and ask, *"If I take you, where will you take me?"* And then they should mentally project into the future and see in their mind's eye where it will take them. It is critical that they take the time to do this.

A number of years ago, Bob Smith Jr., the son of one of the co-founders of Alcoholics Anonymous, spoke at a conference in Vancouver. The son of Bob Sr. and Anne Smith, Bob is well known in addiction recovery circles. At the age of 17, he was present when his father and Bill Wilson (the other co-founder of AA) met for the very first time. Bob Jr. did not become an alcoholic, but he participated in numerous AA, Al Anon, and other recovery events. He shared with us that one of the most profound statements he heard in all of his years of being around the recovery movement came from a speaker at an AA convention whose closing comment was simply, *"Remember this, the person you were will use again."*

I've used those words many times while working with addicts, especially younger ones. In the early stages of recovery, addicts are pre-programmed, when under duress or in crisis, to automatically revert to their old patterns of thinking and acting in response to emotional and environmental cues. As Bob Jr. reminds us, an addict needs to become a different person—a transformation needs to take place—if he or she wishes to avoid relapse.

RELATIONSHIP STRUGGLES

I had a session with a group of young guys who were in their first months of recovery. Several talked about their struggles with relapse. It struck me that their relapse issues were all related to relationships, in particular intimate relationships. It is suggested in recovery circles that if people are new in recovery and not presently in a committed intimate, sexual relationship, then they should stay out of one for the first 15 months. It's critical they keep their focus on their recovery.

If an addict in recovery is in an intimate relationship with a partner who uses drugs, then that is a very treacherous place to be. If the partner is not willing to stop, it may be best for the person in recovery to leave the relationship, at least until his or her recovery is stabilized. If the partner is not using, then the best scenario is for them to get involved in a family support group and attend a family education program. This allows them to better understand themselves in relationship to the addict and be better able to support their partner in recovery.

This group of guys talked about how they have a desperate need to be in an intimate, sexual relationship. They asked what they could do to get through this period of time as it was proving to be challenging. Addicts are both impulsive and compulsive. ***They want what they want when the want it, the way they want it, because that's how they want it, and they don't want it any other way.***

Many young and single adults want to have sex and it's a difficult challenge for them to stay away from it in those critical early months of establishing stable recovery. It just makes sense that people in this situation are best advised to not have sex with others.

A young fellow with a couple of years of recovery told me he'd met a woman who recently started attending his recovery meeting and he was hoping to ask her out. I suggested that he needed to respect *her* recovery and not do anything that would jeopardize it for *her*.

Many people in their first year of recovery hook up with someone from within their recovery meetings and begin a relationship. But chances are, each of them is going to take the focus off his or her own recovery and get swept up in the emotions of the relationship. When this happens, there is a huge danger that it will take them both down. This is because addicts at this stage are not very emotionally mature when it comes to managing relationships. They will be challenged in a sexual relationship by their emotions of obsessiveness, possessiveness, jealousy, a need-to-control, and sense of false ownership. Before they know it they are back thinking and acting as they did when they were using, resulting in a toxic, unhealthy relationship. If this happens, there is a high probability they will go back using again.

Other relationships in the addict's life can also be a downfall. It might be parents, or an immediate family member, or perhaps even a work relationship. When addicts are dealing with relationship problems, they need to focus on recovery and use their support system.

DRY DRUNKS

The term dry drunk has a couple of different meanings. The first occurs when people give up drinking or using, but they don't deal with losing their drug of choice—their 'best friend' and never make it through all the stages of grieving: denial, anger, bargaining, depression, and acceptance. When people don't do the personal work that is needed, they end up staying stuck in resentment, resistance, and anger. They may not have had a drink or used drugs for years, but they have also never known the experience of being happy, joyous, and free.

Dry drunks have been described in various colorful ways including "putting the plug in the jug" and "taking the rum out of the fruit cake, but still being left with fruit cake." Unfortunately, dry drunks can end up angry, miserable, ornery, and impossible to be around. They treat people the same way they did when they were using. Their families and close friends will often say, "He was a terror when he was drinking, but I wish he'd go out and drink again because then at least he'd be some fun."

Secondly, the term dry drunk is used to describe one of the potholes addicts, especially in early recovery, often encounter: a dry drunk *episode*. An episode is when addicts go back to their old emotions, behaviors, and ways of treating themselves and others, especially those closest to them. The only difference now is that they are no longer drinking or using. It can last days, weeks, or months and will generally precede a wet drunk, it is just a question of time. Hopefully, someone having a dry drunk episode will see where he or she is headed and pull out of it before it is too late. Unfortunately, the person often cannot see it. However, if loved ones have participated in a family program, they will almost always recognize the onset of a dry drunk and be able to take appropriate steps and help support the addict through it.

Around 10 months into recovery, I fell into a dry drunk episode that lasted several months. My friend Leroy had warned me that this happens when addicts don't keep the four daily responsibilities in order [don't drink/use that day, be responsible for the health and well-being of self/family, be productive, and maintain a social life] and they forget to watch out for the signs of H.A.L.T. (hungry/angry/lonely/tired).

In my case, Sylvia and I had reconciled after my time at the treatment center, but because I had not sufficiently shaken off my self-centered perspective, I resented the fact that I was now clean and sober but not getting to experience life as a single, sober man. I began to unconsciously shift the four daily priorities, and make my social life my second priority. I thought I had the right to be single and have fun and excitement, and not surprisingly, that effectively put an end to our marriage. Fortunately, with the support of my recovery group and mentor I did not drink or use during this time. I have experienced other dry drunk episodes but that was the most notable.

TWO PERSONALITY TYPES

I've observed in my clinical work that very generally speaking, there are two types of personalities in life, and they show up clearly during recovery—those who are driven to succeed, and those who fear success. There is a real danger period for both personality types between nine and 15 months into recovery. Those psychologically driven to succeed focus on making it to their first year so they can receive the acknowledgement of their recovery group and friends and family for making it to one year clean and sober. Without a further goal, their fervor to succeed subsides, they pull back from being fully active in recovery, complacency sets in, and they relapse, often within weeks of celebrating their first year.

On the other hand, those who fear success will see that one-year milestone looming closer and begin to unconsciously panic, feeling they cannot handle the acknowledgement their achievement is sure to elicit from friends and family. Between the ninth and twelfth month, they unconsciously sabotage their efforts, often relapsing.

I believe that addicts are not on their way to stable recovery until they have entered their fifteenth month of continuous and active recovery. I caution them to work their continuing care program even harder from nine to 15 months, strive to keep the four daily priorities in place, always be conscious of the H.A.L.T. factors, double their number of support meetings, spend more time with their mentors, and work their recovery strictly day by day.

SPIRITUAL DIAPERS

A pastor friend of mine once told me a story about a man he counseled whose life was full of despair. In order to turn his troubled life around, the man had made a commitment to having a personal relationship with God. His life started to change, and he did well for several months before some of his old ways set in again. Fortunately, he came in to see the pastor who listened to his story, then asked how many months it had been since he started his new life. The man said three months, and the pastor responded by gently saying, "Can you see you are still just a baby in this new commitment? You could say you are still wearing your spiritual diapers and now you have soiled them.

"There is nothing wrong with where you are at. Now you have a choice to stay where you are, or clean up and get on with the business of living." The man agreed and the pastor went on to explain, "If you are still messing your diapers after five or ten years then something is desperately missing. We need to address it and figure out what the underlying issues are."

This is great wisdom that can be applied to dry drunks and addiction relapse. If this happens early on, the addict has the choice to clean up or stay in the mess. If someone relapses after a longer time (and that does happen), they need to take a deeper look at what is really going on and address the situation appropriately.

Relapse is so much more complicated today than it was 20 or 30 years ago. Many addicts are now poly-addicted, today's drugs are much more potent, and drugs like crystal meth are highly addictive and highly oriented to relapse.

AND THEN THERE WAS HAROLD

I would be remiss if I didn't mention Harold, a charismatic, happy-go-lucky, single guy who loved booze, drugs, and women. He was always trying to line himself up with women, but because of his addiction, no woman would stay with him for long unless she was equally as addicted. I met Harold shortly after moving to Vancouver as we participated in the same recovery group.

His knowledge of recovery was very impressive. If I was going to speak to somebody who had just reached out for help, and I could have somebody with me, I'd have taken Harold, providing he was sober at the time. He was so knowledgeable and so convincing that the person would surely have listened intently. While he did help scores of people into recovery, he never saw lasting recovery for himself.

Harold was so desperate for attention and recognition that he would do things to give him a single moment in the spotlight. He would make plans to go to a recovery conference, but the day before it began, he would go out drinking. At the conference the chairperson would do a recovery countdown where the individuals with the longest and shortest times in recovery would be asked to come forward. Inevitably the person with the shortest time would be Harold. The chairperson would call him up in front of hundreds, even thousands of people, and he'd receive a standing ovation and steady applause.

I had such admiration for Harold, inside he was a loving spirit who really wanted to help others, but his life wounds had left him extremely confused and emotionally needy. Harold's body was found floating in Vancouver harbor, and no one ever knew what happened.

Most alcoholics, like Harold, are wonderful, caring, sensitive people with big hearts...if you can get them away from the booze and out of their loneliness. It breaks my heart when addicts die prematurely because we lose that wonderful humanity they bring to the world.

Father Martin, an addiction specialist, says that no addict dies in the midst of their disease in vain. Their struggles for recovery pave the way for others who are yet to come behind. I believe this was the case with Harold, my sister Cheri, my niece Patti, and countless others.

CHAPTER SIX

℘

MAINTAINING RECOVERY

It is our attitude at the beginning of a difficult task which,
more than anything else, will affect its successful outcome.

William James, 1842-1910, Psychologist, Professor, and Author

I love the cycles of farming. There is so much to learn from observing the seasons of nature. In the spring we would lightly cultivate the summer fallow field to turn up the rocks so that we could more easily pick them by hand. In those years my relatives didn't own an automated stone picker. If the rocks were big we used crow bars and a front-end loader to take them out. We would pile up the rocks on a stone boat, haul them to a nearby brush area, and unload them, again by hand. When we finished, we'd look out over the field and proudly exclaim, "That there is one good looking field!"

I enjoyed driving the tractor pulling the cultivator and the harrows. In front was a whole mess of weeds, but then I would drive over top and immediately behind me the landscape was transformed. The ever enlarging lines of dark, clean, rich soil created a beautiful picture, and the smell was heavenly. After that, it was time to seed, and then we'd wait patiently while nature took over.

We would stand mesmerized in the summer as we watched fields of golden wheat, barley and oats blowing in the wind. In the fall we reaped the rewards. Winter would come and go, as if the fields had all gone to sleep, and then it was spring—time to again pick the rocks that seemed to pop up from nowhere.

Just like the seasons, life shifts, personal issues surface and we have to clean them up. It's an ongoing cycle as life events continue to challenge us. New people come into our lives, loved ones leave, and we encounter personal or financial trials. For those in recovery these challenges can shake their world.

If people don't deal with these challenges or 'rocks' that appear in the fields of life, they take over and block the ability to know true happiness. When we live in a field of rocks, life becomes difficult—we can no longer grow and develop in love and wisdom. Sometimes we encounter boulders that seem even more grueling to contend with at the time. No matter what they are, we have to be willing to recognize, understand, and clean up our life challenges, seeking outside help if necessary, if we want to grow and reap the rewards life makes available to us.

Maintaining recovery is a process of continually cleaning up life's rocks. In early recovery there are scores of rocks to pick, but as time passes and addicts actively work their recovery, there are fewer rocks. However, the nature of life dictates that there will always be some rocks to contend with.

AN ACT OF SURRENDER

I get a kick out of watching old western movies, especially the scenes where the stagecoach comes thundering across the open prairie. There is one guy driving the horses, and then there is always a second guy riding shotgun who is constantly looking over his shoulder to see who is coming. He is tense, his gun is loaded and ready, and he's prepared to shoot at the first sign of trouble. Active addicts and many in early recovery constantly ride shotgun on the stagecoach of life, while attempting in vain to drive and control it as well. The deeper the addiction and the more trouble addicts get into, the more the intensity of daily life multiplies. It is no wonder that by the time addicts get into recovery, many are so wound up that it's an overwhelming challenge for them to just begin to let go of all the stress.

So the act of surrender becomes critical. Addicts have to stop driving the stagecoach while trying to ride shotgun, and learn to ask for help getting through the experiences they have trouble dealing with. At this stage, recovering addicts should be willing to make a personal commitment to be open to outside support, and do the ongoing work it takes to stay clean and sober. It may mean they need to pray for the very 'willingness to be willing' to accept help and direction.

To admit powerlessness over addiction truly is the gateway or ramp that takes addicts onto the road of recovery. The mere act of surrendering control connects us to a power that is greater than ourselves and our addiction. In this case, surrender is different than merely giving up or giving in—it is about merging with the flow of life and moving in harmony with it.

When we surrender, we don't know how things are going to turn out. Surrender requires an act of faith that involves moving forward without proof. We just let go, turn our situation over to our Higher Power, and do the next right thing, take the next indicated step. It is not about being passive or fatalistic. Surrender involves conscious action. It requires we let go of our attachment to outcomes and place our trust in the process. When we do this, we open ourselves up to possibilities greater than we could have ever imagined or created for ourselves alone.

Steps one, two, and three of 12-step programs can be summarized as: I can't; a power greater than myself can; I think I'll turn it over. It doesn't matter what the addiction is, the first step is to admit one's powerlessness and then turn their life over to a Higher Power of their understanding. And three, "I think I'll turn it over" means I'm going to get out of my own way, quit doing things the way I always have, and stop trying to control everything.

This concept of surrender does not mean someone is no longer responsible for his or her actions or doesn't need to take action. To illustrate this point with recovering addicts, I like to tell the following story.

Around the turn of the last century, an Indian chief asked the local government if he might be deeded some land off the reservation so that he could farm it, and live out his remaining years working the land he loved. The government officials agreed and gave him the deed to a desolate piece of property covered in muskeg, swamp, and quack grass. The chief never complained. He accepted what was, then went to work gathering the tools for the job that lay ahead, a task he realized would take years of work before results were apparent. He got himself an old axe, saw, shovel, rope, a horse, and a plow, and set to work.

One day at a time, he cleared more land, and ensured that what he had already cleared was attended to. He cultivated the soil and planted crops as civilization grew up around him. Over the years his land became the most fertile and lush in the whole valley. One day the local minister came by in his horse and buggy and said to the chief who was busy working his land, "Isn't it wonderful that you have the most fertile piece of land in the whole valley? Isn't it grand what God can do?" The old chief stood up and said, "Yeah, but you should have seen it when He had it all by Himself."

To me this is a story of what can be accomplished when someone takes action and works in harmony with a Higher Power. Recovery doesn't happen in a day, it happens with the willingness and commitment to do the daily work. We have to keep picking up the rocks and clearing the land, so the ground cleaned up in treatment, or on our journey so far, stays fertile. We must always keep in mind that we are working in unison with a Higher Power who is helping us become all we were meant to be. Our Higher Power ensures that we will be provided with the tools to use, we need to pick them up and do the work.

The process of personal growth is difficult because human beings have a natural resistance to change and a desire to keep things just the way they are. To succeed, an addict needs to keep pushing forward. It is like riding a bicycle—it's easy to stay up when you're riding, but difficult to maintain balance while you're standing still. You need to move. By both surrendering and taking action at the same time, movement happens. When you have movement, you have momentum. Once you're moving along on your recovery road, the going gets easier and you get more skilled at riding, but if you get too lazy, complacent, or cocky you *will* fall off.

THE UNSEEN HAND

I discovered early in my recovery that when committing to a journey of personal growth, a Higher Power is there to guide and look after you. People can tell you about it, but you won't really accept it until you experience it first hand. If you simply open yourself up to the possibility, I can guarantee it won't be long before you have proof.

In my second year of recovery, I landed a job as a social worker in Vancouver, and so I moved from Edmonton with great anticipation. Only a few months into the job, the government agency let me go because of a one-year provincial residency requirement for out-of-province social workers that I had been unaware of. I went home that day feeling like the rug had been whipped out from under me, and I didn't know what to do with my feelings of loss, disappointment, and frustration. But before I could get all worked up, my Higher Power quickly saw to it that I would not be alone.

As it happened, a friend who had supported me in my recovery in Edmonton phoned unannounced to say he was in town and wanted to take me out for dinner. We went to a restaurant in Vancouver's Queen Elizabeth Park. It was a beautiful clear evening. The snow glistened as children laughed and tobogganed down the nearby slopes. It was all quite enchanting. When we started dinner I'd been feeling quite sorry for myself, but just talking with my friend made me realize I needed to surrender this situation to my Higher Power, and just act upon those things that were immediately in front of me that I knew I could handle. It was obvious to me by the end of the evening that my friend had not shown up by coincidence, but by the grace of God.

I went home that night, reached into my stack of recovery newsletters and brochures and pulled out one that just had the word EGO on the cover and nothing else. The article asked, "What kind of ego do you want? Used in a negative context," it said, "ego can stand for 'Easing God Out' or 'Edging God Out.'" It also said that it was completely impossible for someone to be resentful and grateful at the same moment. I totally understood that I had a choice to whine and complain about my 'bad luck,' or be thankful for all of the help I'd been given to live my life free of addiction and all the heartache that would have gone with it.

In hindsight, losing that job turned out to be a blessing because it launched me on a different career path leading to where I am today.

MOVING IN HARMONY AND JOY

There is a story of a man who was approached by someone new to recovery who asked, "What is your purpose in life?" Without hesitation, the man replied, "To realize my full potential." When I first heard this I thought to myself, that was nice enough, but what he said next amazed me, and has always stayed with me. He continued, "and to move in harmony with life towards achieving it."

I remember thinking, that's it, that's the key to everything we do. It is not about us. It is about who we are within our environment. It is about harmony, and harmony starts with me. Moving in harmony means I am not operating from a place of selfishness, but that I'm being reasonable, respectful, honest, and fair in all of my dealings in life. Harmony is also about balance, being in tune with what is going on around me and listening to God and to my inner self. This concept was a revelation to me.

Active addicts generally don't have a clue how to live in the joy of the moment because they are always living in the pain of yesterday or in the false hope that things will be better tomorrow. They are often not willing or able to look at being fully accountable and live in the present moment. I don't believe my Higher Power intended that life be more struggle than joy. When we move in harmony, our day-to-day life becomes easier, richer, and much more enjoyable.

Ross, a fellow who ran a recovery home for men, and whom I deeply respect, shared some advice on maintaining recovery that I've never forgotten. He said, "It doesn't matter what people's problems in life are, including if they are an alcoholic or a drug addict. The most important measure of whether you are living life successfully on a daily basis is ***when you walk through the door of the home you live in, are you happy and content, even if you live alone?"***

He explained that if you are not at ease in that situation, regardless of how you present yourself in public, then something's wrong in your life, and you are not moving in harmony with life. He suggested that you had better find what is out of sync for you, engage it, and release it because otherwise it will only get worse, and that is going to lead you back to the place of feeling hungry/angry/lonely/tired. I have always remembered Ross' advice to consciously work on being happy, but haven't always practiced it. It is a great measuring stick to use to help turn your life around and get back on track.

HAPPY, JOYOUS, AND FREE

One of the 12-step recovery programs suggests that when helping others, "Burn into the consciousness of every man that he can get well, regardless of anyone, the only condition is that he trust in God and clean house."

There are two sentiments in this statement that are quite intriguing. The first is the choice of the word 'burn.' From time to time we had to brand the cattle on the farm. Believe me, as soon as that red hot iron hit the animal's hide, it bellowed for all it could. The smell of burning flesh and hair was repulsive. This image of 'burning into the consciousness' is very vivid for me!

The second sentiment is that trusting in God and cleaning house are one condition, not two. Some addicts will try to clean house or clean up the wreckage of the past on their own because they do not want to deal with the God stuff. They avoid it as long as they can and run around partially cleaning house, but it's just a matter of time before their unresolved issues smack them in the face. Strength to maintain recovery comes from learning to trust in a Higher Power and integrating this into one's thinking and belief system.

In recovery circles it is often mentioned that the goal of recovery is to reach a place of being "happy, joyous, and free." This state can only be reached by first learning there is a Higher Power to guide you, by cleaning house, and doing the continuing daily work to keep it clean.

There's a joke that every addict can relate to it. It goes like this: An alcoholic spends the day at the local pub drinking until his money runs out. He stumbles out of the pub just as the engine of a passing car blows up and the car comes to a halt. The driver gets out, lifts the hood up, and checks out the engine. The fellow, quite inebriated, saunters over and says, "Hey buddy, what's the matter?" The driver grumbles, "Damn piston broke," to which the friendly drunk responds, "Me too."

Addicts are often emotionally pissed and spiritually broke. They're not necessarily financially broke, although that might be the case, but they are spiritually broke. In recovery circles this is called being "restless, irritable, and discontent." Another term for this is "being on skid row." Most people think that skid row is a physical place based upon one's economic situation, but every addict, regardless of their position and financial situation in life, knows skid row as an emotional/psychological place based upon their spiritual condition.

In order to reach a place of being happy, joyous, and free, people must address what is spiritually broken—those things that keep them living in a place where they are restless, irritable, and discontent. The hole in the center of their being is a spiritual void that addicts try to fill with alcohol, drugs, work, gambling, sex, food, or whatever they can. These things might temporarily mask the empty feeling, but they won't fix what is broken. The void can be healed only when it is filled with spiritual sustenance—selflessness, service to others, self-respect, and self-love.

GROWING MYSELF UP

A lot of addicts are told by family, friends, and often themselves to "grow up." I was told that many times, even as an adult. It would really upset me because I thought I was already grown up. Some years ago, Kathleen, the therapist I do personal work with said, "Jim, you can take what you are learning and teaching others, and use it to continually help grow yourself up." It was quite a light bulb moment, learning that I could use my life experiences to more meaningfully grow myself up. 'Grow up' is a put down, but 'growing yourself up' is an opportunity. I use this simple phrase when working with others now, and find it to be very powerful.

Recovery involves making mistakes and learning how to resolve difficult situations without going back to drinking or using. It is one way of reprogramming—saying to one's self, "Oh, I guess that doesn't work. Next time I'm going to try doing it differently. And I'm not going to react that way again because I don't like the way it feels." Growing one's self up is about taking risks and leaps of faith. Sometimes people need to let go of a certain way of being or doing things, and try something new and different. Life works best when we just let go and trust the process.

I truly appreciate the clichés often quoted in the various 12-step programs. For example, they say "easy does it"—this is quite different from when we say to someone "take it easy." Taking it easy implies we sit back, relax, and let life happen. But easy does it, speaks to finding the balance, moving forward without overdoing it. Moving forward requires courage—courage is not the absence of fear, it is taking action in the face of it. I've heard it said that fear can stand for "Forget Everything And Run, *or* it can stand for Face Everything And Recover."

Another cliché is "fake it till you make it." A big mistake people in recovery make is to try thinking their way into a new way of acting. I've read that it takes at least 21 days of taking action, or "faking it" for the brain to develop a new way of thinking. Taking action, while finding the balance, is key to growing ourselves up. If people are not moving forward, they are likely moving backward—rarely in life do people just stand still.

Growing and moving forward has everything to do with attitudes and actions. Attitudes will determine actions, and actions reflect attitudes. I believe the term AA stands for much more than Alcoholics Anonymous, it also stands for 'Attitudes and Actions.' If people maintain an easy-does-it but do-it attitude, they will know the right actions to take to move forward in life and to grow themselves up. The life of recovery is conditional upon a person's attitudes and actions, which are driven by his or her spiritual condition.

SIX STEPS TO A DEAL

As a therapist, I ask clients for their willingness to do six things. If they agree, then we have a deal. If they don't I'll tell them I'm not so keen to work with them. I do this for two reasons. First, because I question their commitment to recovery, and second, based on my years of doing clinical work, I believe they'll be less likely to achieve recovery. The six stipulations include:

1. Go to recovery meetings for whatever addiction it is they may be dealing with. They may try several different groups before joining one that feels comfortable. Generally, addicts don't like joining organizations. This is why I insist they begin immediately and go no less than twice a week. The key to maintaining recovery is to become anchored in a support network, whether it is a 12-step group, a faith-based group, or a therapy group. Fellowship with other people who are also on the same quest is critical.

I know addicts who went to residential treatment and decided that was all they needed to do. They believed they didn't need the support of others, nor did they need to do any further work on themselves. They figured that having been through intensive treatment, they now had all this knowledge under their belt, so they could step back, relax and do things their own way. Few of these go-it-alone types are successful long term.

Sticking to a regular schedule of going to support meetings can be a challenge. Those times you don't feel like going to a meeting, and you have all kinds of reasons why you can't go, are when you probably need to go most. It's not until you get to a stage where you really want to go that you can afford to miss a meeting once in a long while.

Some people stop going claiming "they don't *like* the meetings." But *liking* the meetings isn't the issue, *going* is. I've found that once people move beyond this excuse, they do start to enjoy and appreciate the experience.

A recovery group offers tremendous support from others who have lived the same experience and know the pitfalls. Over the 37 years of my recovery, I've made every attempt to attend no less than two such group meetings a week. I cannot emphasize enough the absolute necessity for addicts to pattern their life around recovery and not recovery around their life. In other words, they should not try to fit a meeting in here and there, whenever it works out. Instead they should commit to being at specific meetings and make it work out to be there every time.

2. Join a support group and get active. Go early and set up chairs, make coffee, and do whatever needs to be done for the group. It's about learning how to be in service to others, which is one of the primary keys to achieving contented recovery. In fact research has found that, in general, people who volunteer their time to help others, enjoy a greater sense of personal fulfillment and happiness.

3. Find an interim mentor. I don't ask them to choose their full-time mentor yet because it may turn out their first choice is not going to work out best in the long term. People in early recovery are in an emotionally and socially fragile period of adjustment. It's important that they are able to switch mentors if need be without the emotional worry of having to tell somebody that they wish to work with a different person. It's critical that everyone who enters into recovery has a mentor who is a recovered addict. This helps them develop a support network, and it provides a role model for addicts to start to re-pattern their own lives.

I also strongly recommend the coach or mentor be someone of the same sex, have a minimum of two years active recovery, and that he or she has a solid relationship with their mentor. I also think it is important to find a mentor who used the same drug. A drug is a drug is a drug, but I think a cocaine addict will relate better to another cocaine addict, rather than to an alcoholic because their stories related to using will be similar. I also encourage anyone who had multiple addictions to go to different 12-step groups for each addiction and have mentors for each addiction.

On the negative side, however, I've seen people in recovery get three or four mentors in the same recovery program, and share just a portion of their life with each one. This segmentation is a way of hiding that is quite typical because addicts are uncomfortable and afraid of being hurt or found out. By not telling their whole truth to one person, they make sure no one individual really gets to know them. This doesn't work though because they need that one person to know them intimately, and know their trigger points. They need someone who will go to any length to help keep them working the program.

Leroy, one of my first mentors, got calls from me at all hours of the night. I still value the fact I can make a phone call and connect with someone who knows me inside out. There is no way I could have remained clean and sober over the years without the support of my mentors and coaches.

It is far too easy to relapse in the first few years of recovery without support from an experienced, stable mentor. Four fellows I heard about who were in treatment together all ended up relapsing. Two of them decided, for economic reasons, to get a place together. One of them started using, and not surprisingly, the second fellow started using again as well. The other two guys from treatment went over to help, and all four of them ended up using. Within two months of completing treatment, the four of them were all back where they started.

4. Actively work each of the steps of a 12-step recovery program. Some people think they don't *have* to do the steps, or they can pick and choose the ones they want to do. True, they are suggested—just as it's suggested you pull the ripcord after jumping out of an airplane if you want to save your life. Working the steps involves applying them one by one time in order. I suggest that people look at the steps this way: steps one through three are about putting your trust in a Higher Power, steps four through nine involve, figuratively speaking, cleaning house, and steps eight through 12 require learning about healthy balance and maintenance. You can't do steps four and beyond without having begun the process of letting go and learning to trust in a power greater than yourself. The best way to work the steps is to do so with the support of a 12-step recovery group.

5. Get professional care outside the program, even if it is just for a short time. Some employers offer an Employee and Family Assistance Program, which generally provides counseling at no cost for the employee and family members. I advise people to be very selective and seek out a therapist who understands alcoholism or substance abuse as a primary illness and make sure they follow through on all the recommendations.

I can speak from experience, having spent many hours as a client in counseling sessions myself, that this work has deepened my understanding of who I am, and has pushed me forward on my journey. It is emotional and painful at times, but being heard and understood is uplifting and energizing. Many times my counselor has been able to help me identify the direction I needed to take on the next step of my journey, when I couldn't see it for myself.

6. Develop or continue to work on spiritual growth and a relationship with a Higher Power, as they understand it to be. Some people choose not to because of their feelings around the concept of a Higher Power, but they are willing to work on their self-worth, pride, and dignity. This is okay too because it is a significant part of spiritual growth. Spiritual growth is difficult. It demands introspective searching and a realignment of one's values and beliefs. I put spiritual growth last on my list of six, not because it's the least important, but rather because it's what supports people in working on the first five requirements. It is the foundation upon which sustained recovery must be built.

I work with addicts to set up a complete plan before they do anything else. They need to know who to contact when they get out of treatment and who might be willing to act as their interim mentor, and they also need to get set up with a counselor for any continuing clinical support they might need. A solid two-year continuing care program is absolutely critical to avoid relapsing. Again, it is important to remember that relapse begins well before a person picks up a drink or drug—it starts when they fail to follow their continuing care process. The act of using is the final stage of relapse. My friend and colleague Neal Berger says, "If addicts are not actively involved in their recovery, the default position is always relapse."

When someone has an operation for cancer or heart disease, they will complete a continuing care program. This generally entails a change in lifestyle to maintain good health and ensure this type of illness does not come back. Addiction is just the same—a change in lifestyle is necessary for success.

12 STEPS IN PERSPECTIVE

I admit that in my clinical and professional view I am unabashedly an advocate for 12-step programs. In my experience they are more effective than anything else because they provide a succinct and ongoing plan for recovery. There *are* addicts who successfully achieve sobriety participating in recovery programs or processes that do not incorporate the traditional 12-steps; however I believe working the steps significantly increases one's chances. There are now 12-step programs for virtually any life challenge you can think of, and such programs are found all over the world for good reason...they get results and cost nothing.

But at the same time, many people do relapse. Why? In the 12-step recovery process there are two components: the program or working the steps, and the fellowship. People are more likely to relapse if they don't get engaged quickly enough in the actual script of recovery, and don't work each step in sequence, the way they are intended to be worked. Instead, those who relapse generally find themselves participating too much in the fellowship and social aspects of recovery, and that doesn't treat the disease. These people get caught up in talking about the external circumstances of their life, but they aren't addressing their addiction and the spiritual malady that need to be healed. It's often the case that these people place themselves in social situations outside the program that are a slippery place for their recovery.

On the other hand, the social aspects of the program are extremely important so that people don't get dragged down by loneliness. It's a question of balance between working the steps which provide an opportunity to address all the issues impacting one's life, and using the recovery program to help establish a strong and healthy social network.

There are always a few exceptions. Some people do stay off alcohol and drugs by participating in the fellowship without working the steps. But I question whether they have achieved a state of being happy, joyous, and free. I believe it takes a relationship with a Higher Power to keep a recovering addict sober during the tough times, to help maintain balance, and be able to realize contentment in life.

Working the steps will bring someone to a point of finding that relationship with a Higher Power where it is possible to address the spiritual malady. The 12th step of these programs promises that people with addictions will have a spiritual awakening as a result of doing the work. It is through doing the steps that one begins to make a conscious connection to their Higher Power. The fellowship enriches lives and provides the support needed when working the steps. It is this combination that brings recovery to millions of addicts around the world.

Many people classify 12-step programs as self-help programs. They are not. If addicts could do it themselves they would. These programs are spiritual programs. They involve a process of taking action that allows participants to heal through a relationship with a Higher Power.

Of all of the chronic, terminal diseases in the world today, addiction has the greatest potential of full reprieve because of this process. If you told people who had cancer that you can guarantee they would be totally cancer free if they were to spend two to three hours a week attending some pretty interesting and fun meetings, and taking some action that would bring them closer to their Higher Power, I imagine that many would jump at the chance. Recovery from addiction is relatively straight-forward. Unfortunately, many people suffering from addiction or the addiction of a loved one cannot see this, or they refuse to see it.

CHAPTER SEVEN

℘

CONTINUED, CONTENTED RECOVERY

One day at a time is enough. Do not look back and grieve over the past, for it is gone; and do not be troubled about the future, for it has not yet come. Live in the present, and make it so beautiful that it will be worth remembering.

Ida Scott Taylor, 1820-1915, Author

I love the idea of recovery being a journey because it really is akin to traveling down a long and winding road where travelers may need to negotiate copious hills, curves, potholes, and perhaps even craters along the way. At the same time, the journey is filled with profound learning and new experiences that bring a sense of accomplishment and joy. While I believe the road of recovery has no final destination, in the sense that there is always more to learn, the road can lead us to a place of finding our true inner self where we experience inner peace, love, and trust.

When Leroy reminded me in my early months, "If you plan to obtain and maintain any degree of continued, contented recovery, you will attempt to attend no less than two support meetings a week for the rest of your life," I could not begin to go there in my head. My whole focus was on obtaining and maintaining recovery one day at a time. The concept of contentment was beyond me—so was thinking about the rest of my life.

Making the journey from discontentment to contentment takes considerable effort. Contentment comes when we are comfortable with ourselves and the way things are in our life. Contentment allows us to freely embrace our physical, mental, and spiritual self.

When we find the path to self-acceptance and self-love we find our *authentic* self. By this I mean recognizing and celebrating all those things about us that make us unique as individuals. When we discover our authentic selves, we begin to feel complete, the hole in our spirit fills up. This is when we start to feel whole and at peace with who we are in the world.

A FOCUS ON VALUES

A large part of being authentic has to do with identifying and living one's values. I learned about living according to one's values from my mother early on in my life. Values are the standards or principles that are most important to us. To this day, my mom lives by the value of steadfast faith. She has absolute faith that God will take care of us when we ask.

I recall a time when I was 10 years old, the only food in the house to feed my mom and five kids was a big box of macaroni. With only 10 dollars to buy food until my dad returned from working out-of-town, she still gave 10 percent of her grocery money to the church. I remember being so angry at the time that the church, knowing how poor we were, would take her money. Even though it wasn't much, it was still 10 percent of what little we had.

For my mom, there was no question that she would give what she could to the church to help others in need. She had absolute faith that God would take care of our family. She lived her life based on this value. Looking back, I realize that while we didn't have much, we never starved.

Many of the values that shape who I am today came from the time spent living on the farm in rural Saskatchewan. In a time of need, everyone—Catholics and Protestants, believers and non-believers, conservatives and socialists, would put aside their differences, and drop whatever they were doing in order to come to someone's aid, all in the spirit of community.

I remember watching a dozen or more farmers assemble one of those pre-fabricated steel quonset huts in a modern day barn-raising. My uncle bought it to house the tractor and other equipment knowing there would be lots of available hands to help put it together. At lunchtime, the men's wives all showed up with food for everyone. It didn't matter what their faith or political beliefs were, or that they might have something more pressing to do on their own farm, they came to help out. Inevitably, the day was filled with laughter and camaraderie.

Another time my uncle's hay stack caught on fire. The hay had been damp when it was baled and stacked, and three days later, because of the moisture, spontaneous combustion set it off. When the fire erupted, my aunt got right on the old party-line phone, gave it the general ring, and within 10 minutes a half-dozen farmers arrived, quickly extinguishing the fire and saving the old barn. This spirit of community proved to be a unique and invaluable form of insurance. It was simply understood that if trouble should befall any one, their neighbors would be there to help out, no matter what. They all lived by the value of being in service to each other, especially in times of need.

I often reflect on how life can be like that hay stack sometimes —all looks good on the outside, but inside things are heating up with a force that becomes explosive. People often get so focused on looking good, being right, keeping secrets, and not being completely honest that they lose sight of their authentic self. Then, when life challenges hit, just like when fresh air hits an open pocket and gets into the center of the hay stack, everything just explodes with an intense destructive force.

Another lesson I received, related to living one's values, occurred during my month at the treatment center. I became friends with Jack, a successful business man in his mid-forties. I quite liked him. He was easy-going and fun to be with and we played many leisurely hours of cribbage. Despite earning good money in the real estate business, the Sheriff's department came to the center and towed away his brand new two-door Chrysler Newport hardtop. He wasn't too bothered about it at all saying that when he got out of treatment he would just declare bankruptcy and start over. Knowing that I owed a lot of money, he suggested that I should do the same. Declaring financial bankruptcy was a foreign concept to me. It was June of 1972 and I owed $15,000 which was a lot of money at that time, considering I was only making $65 a week. But I had no intention of bailing out.

I knew intuitively that if I declared financial bankruptcy, I would also be declaring bankruptcy emotionally and spiritually. I couldn't afford to do that. I had made a commitment to everyone I owed money to, including my mom, to whom I owed $6,000 at the time. It wasn't their problem that I'd blown so much money on booze and drugs. It took me about five years, but I did pay back every cent I owed.

Jack declared bankruptcy soon after he left treatment. Within a few months he got on a high roll again and it wasn't long before he started smoking dope and then drinking. In less than two years he was dead. Although I could not have articulated it at the time, this was a lesson for me that recovery meant living life with integrity. When we live by the value of integrity we are honest and open in all our dealings, and we honor and respect ourselves and all others in our life.

FOUR VIRTUES

If recovery is to be successful, people must be willing to fully commit to cleaning up the wreckage of their past (the past could be yesterday or many years ago). That stuff needs to get cleaned up or it gets carried around like baggage that just weighs a person down and makes it difficult to obtain and maintain continued, contented recovery. I believe we can be greatly supported in the process by working on four qualities or virtues: forgiveness, trustworthiness, honesty, and gratitude.

Addicts are focused so intently on their own wants and desires they become like young children whose perception is that the world revolves around only them. I read a booklet years ago called *King Baby* and the title always makes me chuckle. It's so appropriate because addicts do almost anything to get what they want, when they want it.

In their early recovery, addicts often feel resentful towards different people, institutions, and events in their life—sometimes pursuing their resentment to the point of obsession. They have to learn to release their narcissistic way of looking at the world and quit seeing themselves as a victim or it will destroy their recovery. Resentment is an unaffordable attitude, addressing it early through *forgiveness* is at the core of recovery.

When addicts forgive themselves and others, they can then begin to release their resentments, make amends, and experience peace of mind. But unless they let go of their grievances, the emotional links will bind them to those persons or conditions and they cannot feel free. Errors are part of being human, forgiveness erases errors and leads to freedom.

Most addicts feel victimized: "It should never have happened to them, they aren't at fault, they are owed." Recovering addicts have to move out of the victim role of believing that people, places, or things have done certain injustices to them causing pain. Victims don't get sober. They may get dry for a period of time but they don't find true sobriety. Instead of projecting blame, they have to look at their own responsibility, and even more so, their own accountability and ask themselves how their actions contributed to each event that has angered or hurt them. Then they need to look at forgiving themselves as well as others.

In order to forgive themselves, addicts have to know that God not only forgives, but forgets their 'mistakes.' Whatever it was they did, as far as their Higher Power is concerned, it no longer exists. When I first got sober, I thought God would not forgive me for the things I had done during the years of my active using. It wasn't that I had done anything that serious, but I still feared the God of my evangelical upbringing. It took three or four years to let go of that baggage and see my Higher Power as an all-loving presence in my life.

Forgiveness is such a powerful tool. At some point, we must make a choice to let go of our judgments, anger, and fear in favor of understanding, compassion, and love. It is then that we start to know true peace of mind.

Another area that causes difficulty for addicts is the issue of *trust*. When I was drinking, I would often lie to my mother and manipulate her in order to get my own way. I knew she loved me, but I just did what I did nevertheless. She knew she couldn't trust me but she loved me with all her heart, so she would come and bail me out of jail when she should have left me there. Addicts know how to abuse trust to gain advantage. Of course it's not long before those we abuse no longer consider us trustworthy.

A quote I once read in Readers Digest stated that, "It is greater to be trusted than to be loved." Another quote I recall reading is "Trust is the highest form of human motivation." There is no question that trust resides at the core of all healthy, harmonious relationships. Without trust, our relationships are filled with suspicion, defensiveness, protectiveness, disrespect, and, at times, deceit. If people can't count on us being there for them, how can we have open, honest relationships?

Regaining someone's trust and becoming trustworthy takes time and patience. Trust needs to be rebuilt gradually through the course of personal interactions by demonstrating that we are dependable, that we keep our word and our commitments, and that we can be accountable for our actions. It often requires consciously working on forgiveness, courage, honesty, and self-responsibility. Trust will not be granted again once it has been broken, it must be earned back.

Active addicts are notorious for lying, manipulating, and telling only partial truths. How can you tell an addict is lying? Their mouth is moving! It's a well-known joke about addicts which brings us to the virtue of *honesty*. Addicts not only tell lies, they often live a lie—presenting themselves to others, especially those who love and care deeply about them, as though living one way when they are not. Telling a lie can be harmful to everyone; however, living a lie eats you up and eventually destroys the spirit. You can't obtain and maintain recovery if you continue to tell lies or live a lie.

Addicts in recovery must learn to work continually at telling the truth at all times to all people. Their personal interactions need to be clean and clear.

Recovery groups talk about the need for 'rigorous' honesty, not just 'cash-register' honesty, but honesty in how you live your whole life. To be completely honest with others, you must first be completely honest with yourself. The energy it takes to keep secrets and tell lies is much greater than the energy it takes to be open and honest!

Many people, not just addicts, opt for a life of limited honesty and openness, and thus they never find that place of being happy, joyous, and free. I am reminded of the biblical saying, "And you shall know the Truth, and the Truth shall set you free." Truth has an amazing quality of lightness, while lies or untruths feel heavy. If you shine the light of truth on any difficult situation, the feelings of anxiety fade away. Darkness cannot prevail when you shine a light on it. Intentional deception or dishonesty about ourselves or our world is not an option when we work at being rigorously honest.

Gratitude is the fourth virtue that helps pave the road to contentment. I mentioned earlier that it is completely impossible to be resentful and grateful at the same time. How do we express gratitude to those whom we feel have hurt or betrayed us? How do we get to a place of appreciating the lessons we learned in our relationships with them? I think the answer lies in understanding that almost always, people do the best they can with what they have been given in life.

I find that when difficulties arise in my life, I need to stop and ask myself, "What is the lesson in this for me?" When you look with an open heart at what is going on in your life, the lesson or gift becomes obvious. Then, when you can give thanks in the middle of your trials, you can move forward. Adopting an 'attitude of gratitude' can be transformative. But it's also important to remember that gratitude is more than a feeling, it requires action. When we are grateful, we appreciate what we have received, and we demonstrate it or express it in some way. Bill W., one of the founders of AA, is quoted as saying that gratitude is the hinge upon which the door of recovery swings.

Developing and cultivating the virtues of forgiveness, trustworthiness, honesty, and gratitude are all critical elements in finding contented recovery.

MAKING OUR AMENDS

When we talk about doing the *work* of recovery, much of that work involves making amends. The process of making amends in recovery requires dealing with the hurts and harms we caused others as well as ourselves throughout our life. In a 12-step program, it is described in step eight: "Made a list of all persons we had harmed, and became willing to make amends to them all," and step nine: "Made direct amends to such people wherever possible, except when to do so would injure them or others."

Often people wish they hadn't done certain things in the past, but it's impossible to wish them away. Accepting what was done and owning up to it can be painful to face, but until this is done, the guilt, resentment, shame, or remorse of it just simmers in the unconscious and prevents healing from taking place.

Making amends means taking full responsibility for our part in any past wrongs. Where possible, addicts need to talk with the people and institutions they may have hurt, cheated, or lied to, and listen with patience and without judgment as they describe for us how they feel. As they listen, they need to put themselves in the other person's shoes and accept that this is his or her truth. Then they need to find out if and how they can make the relationship right again. Saying we're sorry is not enough—healing comes from the willingness to ask for forgiveness from those we harmed, and where applicable, make full restitution.

If a person who was harmed is unwilling to forgive, that is his or her right. It is between this individual and God—our part is done. The important thing is that we forgive ourselves and know that we have done what we needed to in order to fully make our amends.

When preparing to make amends, it can be helpful to consult with a spiritual advisor and one's mentor. Step five of 12-step programs state that people must admit to God, to themselves and to another human being the exact nature of their wrongs. I once organized a workshop solely on the fifth step for a number of religious leaders from various faiths. It proved to be an enlightening experience for these clergy people as they discovered their role in helping addicts do their critical work.

Addicts in recovery also need to look at what secrets they may be harboring. There is a saying that behind every relapse is a secret. Our secrets can be our own worst enemy, so dealing with our secrets becomes part of cleaning up the past. Recovery programs recommend keeping in mind H.O.W.—honesty, openness, and the willingness to take action. Sometimes the wrongs of our past include times where we secretly hurt ourselves, perhaps self-mutilation or suicide attempts, and so we may need to forgive ourselves as well as others.

When addicts start cleaning up the wreckage of their past, they experience a profound sense of freedom. When they feel free and complete with the past, they attract more positive situations and enjoy life more fully. A spiritual healing takes place when making amends.

BEING IN SERVICE

Someone pointed out to me recently how interesting it is that the word *illness* begins with "I" and the word *wellness* begins with "we." As discussed, addicts are always self-centered and preoccupied with their own issues. For addicts to become well again, it is critical they learn to take the focus off themselves and work their recovery with the support of other people.

In order to maintain and achieve contented recovery, addicts, once they are involved doing the work of recovery and using their mentor, need to "give it away." They have to begin giving support back to others — in other words, go from a focus of "I" to a focus of "we".

When you help other people, you soon begin to feel better. Helping others provides an amazing opportunity to discover whom we really are and what we are capable of doing. I've found that when I've had my 'cheeks puckered down on the pity pot of life' in a 'poor Jim' attitude, by doing something for someone else, I take the attention off me and my perception of the severity of my problems. By being in service, addicts in recovery can transcend their problems and their selfishness, and achieve a greater sense of well being.

I have in my possession a photocopy of a prescription written in February 1937 by Dr. Bob Smith, one of the co-founders of Alcoholics

Anonymous, which he wrote for individuals suffering from alcoholism. Dr. Smith's prescription was simply this, "***Trust God, clean house, and help others.***"

Helping others is one of the fundamental principles of recovery fellowships. When we work with others, we can't help but learn something about ourselves in the process. Recovery programs understand this, they know there is an obligation—a spiritual obligation—to help those who are new to the recovery process. People in recovery and family members sometimes ask when will the debt to recovery be repaid. You cannot set a timeframe on the recovery process. It needs to be viewed as a life-long act of service. The more people continue to help others, the more they deepen themselves and their recovery.

But there are potential pitfalls to helping others. I've always appreciated this piece of advice for those who act as mentors. "***You are not there to make them do it, you are there to help them through it.***" It is easy to get carried away by always being the Good Samaritan, and end up with 'big shoulderitis.' If you've been rescued from living a life of hell in your addiction, it is natural to feel a strong debt of gratitude and want to rush out to help someone else in trouble. However, you must ensure you are not doing for others what they need to be doing for themselves.

I love the story of the man with a compassionate heart who, while out walking in nature, stops to observe a butterfly desperately trying to free itself from its cocoon. In a moment of compassion, he decides to help and carefully slits open the cocoon. The young butterfly spreads its beautiful wings, struggles briefly and then dies. It is the very struggle of the butterfly to free itself from the cocoon that forces blood into its wings and gives it life. The struggles in our lives are no different. There are times we need to allow others to work through their difficulties and not rescue them, although we can be there to support them.

Being too overzealous when it comes to helping others can become a place to hide out. People can get so caught up helping others they forget to spend time focusing on their own personal growth work. With those words of caution, I do believe we are here to be in service to our fellow travelers on this earth.

To keep recovery you have to give it away by helping others—this is a spiritual principle. Helping others keeps the spiritual part of us connected, alive, and rejuvenated. We can't live off the food we ate a week ago, our nutritional sustenance needs to be kept up. The same is true for recovery. Helping others is spiritual sustenance, and at the same time, contributes to making the world a more compassionate and caring place.

LIVING IN INTEGRITY

When my colleagues and I do workshops on substance abuse in the workplace, we ask participants to identify their values—those principles, standards, or qualities that they hold as most desirable or worthwhile. They come up with a list that includes values such as ensuring honest and open communications, fairness in all dealings, keeping promises, and being respectful. We then ask them to identify their behaviors in relation to the problem addict in the workplace, and they tell us how they might do the addict's work for them, turn a blind eye, cover-up, lie, or any number of behaviors meant to keep the addict out of trouble. Finally, we ask participants if these behaviors are in sync with their personal values. We hear a lot of moaning as the mental light bulbs flicker on and people realize how they are not being consistent, in this and other areas of their lives.

We maintain personal integrity by constantly measuring our behavior against our values. As the gap widens between what we say we value and how we live our lives, we lose integrity, our personal effectiveness decreases, and we inevitably experience internal anxiety.

When addicts are in the midst of their addiction, values they hold as being important, such as family relationships or meaningful work, get hijacked by their illness. Most addicts are unaware of how addiction has become the focal point of their lives around which everything else revolves. In recovery, they have to replace addiction with values that are most important to them. When they start living these core values, they begin to live a life of integrity.

Core values can be regarded as spiritual principles that we strive to live by. I highly recommend that people take the time to identify and write down their core values—what is most important to them and what it is they stand for in this life. They should then put this list where it can be reviewed each morning and assessed at the end of each day.

When we 'walk our talk' and live from a foundation of principles, we experience a sense of fulfillment, peace, and authenticity.

"I CAN LOVE MYSELF."

The process of recovery is often described as selfish, not in the sense of being totally absorbed with your own material well-being, but in the sense of taking care of your emotional, mental, physical, and spiritual health first, before anyone else. It is like traveling on an airplane with a small child—if the oxygen masks drop down, you are clearly instructed to put yours on first, before taking care of the child.

As we begin to operate from our core values and to develop our virtues, a complete psychic shift starts to happen, and we begin to accept and appreciate ourselves. As we continue to work on our relationship with a Higher Power, we begin to discover who we really are at our core. We feel excited about being in the world because we no longer see it as a scary place. We move forward in our recovery, appreciating that we can make it, that there are opportunities for us, and that there is hope for a better life.

One of the great things I learned from all of the workshops and seminars, books, and therapy, is to really love Jim. Learning to love myself involved getting to know and accept myself, and trust that the things in me that needed to change would get changed.

When we love ourselves, and know that our Higher Power loves us, then we can truly love others—our spirit opens up and our heart is more willing to be present to others. When we get to a place in our journey where we honestly can declare that we love ourselves, we are able to extend unconditional love to others. It's a major milestone when people say they truly love themselves. Much of society would have us believe that love is external to us, and we need to look outside of ourselves for it. But love first has to start inside one's self.

Self-love allows us to self scrutinize and learn how to accept our weaknesses and our strengths. This is the essence of true humility. I had the honor to work with Dr. George Strachan, a giant in the addictions field in Canada. He would say that "true humility is teach-ability." By this, he meant we need to be willing to be a student of life, always open to new ideas. As we progress through recovery, there are constant opportunities for learning and growing. The more we are open, the more we will learn and grow.

RECOVERED OR RECOVERING?

People ask me whether I am a 'recovering' addict or a 'recovered' addict. I reply that I am recovered. For me, this implies that I have reached a place in the work of recovery where I know that I am valued, that I have a meaningful relationship with a Higher Power, and that I can love me. However, I'm still an addict because I know if I were ever to use again, it would not take much for me to return to feeling restless, irritable, and discontent. Doing the personal work of recovery on an ongoing basis allows a person to transition from a recovering to a recovered addict. When that line is crossed is a very individual process. But while someone may have achieved a fair degree of contentment and self-respect, recovery cannot be taken for granted. Recovery is a daily reprieve from a life-threatening illness.

I am proud of my sobriety. The word sobriety means much more than being dry, which implies the absence of alcohol in the body's system. Alcoholics are often 'dry' some of the time. Sobriety is a way of living and it requires a complete shift or change of our psyche. You don't achieve it overnight—it's a long process and you can lose it quickly if you fail to do the maintenance. Sobriety involves a complete transformation that brings with it a sense of contentment and peace, and in time allows one to experience a state of truly being happy, joyous, and free.

When I was in my fourth year of recovery, someone asked me what being happy in recovery meant to me. Without thinking about it, I reached into my pocket and pulled out my set of keys and said, "Here is the key to my home. When I was drinking, my wife (Sylvia) on occasion locked me out at night and I had to find a place to spend the night. Now I know I can always go home. This is my car key. When I was drinking I lost my license and had my car taken from me on a number of occasions. That is not a worry for me anymore. This is the key for my work. When I was drinking, my employers would never trust me to have a key to my place of employment. That is no longer an issue. To me, these keys represent the happiness, joy, and freedom I now have in my life."

It is often quoted in the recovery arena that recovery may not open the gates of Heaven to let you in, but it definitely opens the gates of Hell to let you out. This is true. But I also believe that as we work our recovery, the gates of Heaven, figuratively speaking, do open for us.

CHAPTER EIGHT

෨

RECOVERY AND RELATIONSHIPS

For one human being to love another; that is perhaps the most difficult of all our tasks, the ultimate, the last test and proof, the work for which all other work is but preparation.

Rainer Maria Rilke, 1875-1926, German Poet

Three months after my sister Cheri died I started to question where I was at in my own life. Her life and death at only 44 years of age triggered an epiphany that felt like a cannon ball blasting across the bow of my life. I asked myself if I were to die tomorrow would I leave this world feeling satisfied, fulfilled, and at peace? My answer was no. I had 25 years of continuous sobriety at that point. I believed I had done everything I could to achieve contentment, but something was still missing.

On the surface I had it all—a lovely and loving wife, two great kids (both teenagers at the time), and a job where I could make a difference in people's lives. Despite this, I realized there was a void in my life that I'd been filling up with activities. I concluded that my 20-year marriage was not where I needed it to be. In my confusion and search to fill the void, I had a short-lived affair, which wasn't the answer of course. Within a year of Cheri's death, I left my marriage.

This was an exceedingly gut-wrenching time in my life. I knew what I was doing was very tough on my wife Anne and our two boys, and I experienced enormous guilt and shame. There were times when the pain was so deep and I was so filled with grief I would cry uncontrollably. This was, without question, the most painful period of my life, but it was also a time of profound, deep soul-searching.

What I learned during this time is also what I believe to be one of the last phases of recovery: to reach a place of being at peace with your Higher Power and yourself, and to take that into a love relationship where one can experience a sacred place of intimacy and communion with another human soul. Kathleen, the therapist I worked with told me she believed the ability to attract and maintain a long-term intimate relationship was the last frontier of emotional maturity for most addicts. She suggested that doing the work of creating healthy relationships can be harder for some people than quitting alcohol or drugs.

CHILDHOOD WOUNDS

Growing up in a home with an addicted parent(s) definitely impacts our ability to attract and maintain a loving relationship as an adult. For example, a child, let's say a young girl, gets up out of bed and goes downstairs. Mom is already up, and passing by the front window, the girl sees her dad sleeping on the front lawn with a blanket and pillow. The child's inner alarm sounds. Mom is agitated and Dad is sleeping on the lawn. Mom says that Dad is camping, and mutters something about being embarrassed. She had locked the door and left a blanket and pillow outside when he didn't come home from work, yet again. Mom says that everything is fine and sends the girl upstairs to play. When the child tries to find out what is going on, Mom explodes and the girl runs to her room upset, feeling she is somehow to blame for the situation. When Mom hears the child crying, she yells, "Stop crying or I'll give you something to cry about!"

What do children take away from situations like this? First, they learn not to trust. Mom obviously lied about the situation and invalidated the child's feelings. Next, children learn that they are not to talk about such situations openly and honestly. Finally, they learn not to acknowledge their feelings—that it is not acceptable to show emotions. The family develops unspoken, usually dysfunctional rules which somehow allow them to exist together.

Children raised in dysfunctional homes don't know that life can be different. The traits they learn in order to survive are etched into the characters of the adults they become. This behavior pattern moulds their attitudes, actions and reactions, especially behaviors that involve love and intimacy in relationships. The very responses that once helped these children survive become roadblocks as they attempt to establish meaningful relationships later on.

It's important to remember you can only give away what you were given. If you were raised in the home of an addict, or with sexual abuse, then you will likely attract experiences to you using the magnet of your upbringing. Changing that magnet requires that you heal your past and change your thinking and behaviors.

However, changing your thinking and learned behaviors require conscious, focused work—work that is challenging and emotionally charged, but extremely rewarding. Being honest, open, and trusting, for example, may not have been safe things to do in a dysfunctional family, but they need to happen for a relationship to be healthy.

My wife Anne and I both grew up with fathers who were chemically dependent, and we each carried our own issues of don't talk about feelings, don't tell the whole truth, and my favorite, keep the peace at all costs. What was the chance of our marriage surviving, even if I didn't drink, when we had not fully dealt with these core issues? Probably pretty slim. Inevitably, the results of these behaviors are going to come to the forefront of the marriage. While there was mutual respect and love, and little anger or disruption in our marriage, we didn't have the passion (from my perspective) that comes from speaking our truth and sharing who we are at our core. A passionate, empowered relationship can only come from sharing our deepest feelings. Yet all of the instincts molded by our childhood tell us to do the opposite: don't talk, don't feel, and don't trust.

We stayed together because of our strong mutual respect and spiritual commitment, our children, and other responsibilities. We carried on and certainly did have many good years together. I would not have wanted to live this life without having known and loved Anne, to have been her partner, and to have experienced the joy of our two boys.

Were we doomed from the beginning? I don't think so. Perhaps it was akin to the mechanic whose car keeps breaking down, but he never gets around to properly fixing it because he's so busy with his customers' and friends' cars. As someone who counsels other people in recovery and relationship matters, one would think that I should have known sooner what to do. Over the years we attended a few relationship retreats, and I recall one facilitated by a priest who said that in the process of life as a couple, if you are not growing together, you are growing apart. If this continues, then at some point there is a big schism between you. In hindsight, I can see why my marriage ran into problems. Anne and I had not done the work needed to heal our childhood wounds.

Based on my experiences working with scores of addicts, I believe that most of them have a deep-seated yearning to attract and maintain a long-term, deep, meaningful love relationship. I don't know if this is any different from the general population, but I do know that this is one thing that addicts are often completely incapable of creating. Most often this is directly related to issues with their family of origin, and also to the fact that their own drug abuse may have messed up their ability to effectively handle their emotions. As addicts move through recovery and become aware of their feelings, deep-seated fears can be reawakened. But wounds can be healed and loving relationships are possible for anyone who is willing to do the work.

It's said that we should love our neighbor as ourselves. Interesting, isn't it? The one thing addicts don't know how to do is love themselves, so how can they truly love their neighbor? In addiction, and even before that, the whole subject of love is confusing. And for addicts, as for many others, love, sex, and relationships often get confused.

GROWING UP IN RELATIONSHIPS

After my second marriage ended, I threw myself into doing personal development work. I devoured books on personal and spiritual growth, and I undertook some innovative in-depth therapy sessions of neurofeedback where a therapist hooked me up to probes to help rewire some very specific parts of my brain circuitry. I was determined to do everything I could to figure out why I didn't feel satisfied and fulfilled at this stage of my life.

One of the therapists I worked with at this time asked, "Jim, have you ever had somebody reach deep inside of you and touch a place of passion?" I didn't understand the meaning of passion because I hadn't yet learned about the depth of loving myself. He explained, "When someone very special reaches deep within you at the right time, and in the right circumstances, awakening the place called passion, your soul will not rest until it is anchored in an intimate, soulful relationship. You will know passion in a new and deeper way. That person may not end up being your soulmate for life, but the realization of what is possible will stay with you forever."

This therapist went on to say that if this passion awakens in you, consider yourself very fortunate because many people go through life without ever feeling true passion. But when it does happen, you have the opportunity to make great strides in your emotional and spiritual growth.

My affair did not last long, but my desire for passion was awakened more deeply than ever before. A wise elderly friend put it into context for me when she said, "Jim, can you see that this woman who came across your path at that time in your life was really a midwife, and not the person you were supposed to be with? In essence, what you went through was a form of rebirthing, moving you from a place where your soul was not awakened, to a place where you could stretch your wings?"

What has become clear to me is that learning to love one's self is a critical leg of the journey. The more we like and have respect for ourselves, the more we can extend love to others. It is in the process of loving others that we learn and come to understand even more about ourselves as we grow ourselves up in life. It's a process that can't happen in isolation. Relationships, especially intimate love relationships, are an extraordinary opportunity to learn about ourselves, to work through those places in us that still need healing, and to learn about the needs of the soul.

ESTABLISHING HEALTHY BOUNDARIES

I am not a relationship counselor, and I certainly don't want to profess that I am any kind of expert in this area, but I have observed myself and other addicts in relationships, and I've noticed several areas where we struggle. One important area is that of setting personal boundaries. Addicts don't understand personal boundaries—their own or others. Generally, we learn about boundaries in the home where parents set fair and reasonable limits and parameters for their children and for themselves. But the majority of addicts come from homes with some level of dysfunction where healthy boundaries were not taught or modeled. This is not about blaming parents, as they too likely came from homes with some degree of dysfunction.

Establishing personal boundaries means accepting that we are separate individuals with our own emotions, needs, attitudes, and values. With healthy boundaries we are able to tell others how we want to be treated in a relationship, and discern when our partner is acting in ways that are not acceptable to us. It may even mean that we practice detachment, releasing someone with love, if necessary.

Establishing healthy boundaries requires that we learn to be honest with ourselves, and then learn to communicate in a direct and sincere way. A good rule to remember is to "Say what you mean, mean what you say, and don't be mean about it." For example, you might need to say something like, "No, I cannot do that (fill in the blank) with you as I need time by myself right now. But you are important to me, so I will do it, or talk about it later."

For the addict setting clear boundaries can be as daunting a task as flying a space shuttle to the moon. It wasn't until I was in my thirties that I started to understand more deeply the concept of boundaries

—mine and others. Even now I'm not sure I am always that adept at establishing and maintaining my personal boundaries.

For someone in recovery who has not learned about boundaries, it becomes easy to lose sight of what you want for you and become enmeshed with other people. Of course, where that really shows up is in intimate relationships. If you can't *do* boundaries, you will likely burn out and may relapse. The challenge for addicts is to be responsible and accountable to themselves so that they honor themselves and preserve their integrity.

When we have healthy boundaries, we can be intimate with others because we feel there is control in our lives, and we know we have a choice about what we will or won't accept from others, as well as from ourselves. The key, as I am still learning, is to clearly and consistently assert one's own boundaries so that they are clear to others. At the same time we want to be aware and respectful of other people's boundaries.

UNBLOCKING FEELINGS

Another area of relationships where people struggle is in expressing feelings. Drug and alcohol dependency injures our physical, mental, emotional, and spiritual selves. That being the case, recovery must occur on different levels for each of these parts to be healed. Physical recovery occurs when the body's physical needs are cared for. Mental recovery happens as the brain is rewired when addicts shift their attitudes, beliefs, and ways of thinking. Emotional recovery takes time and effort. It starts to happen as addicts learn to deal with feelings in an open, honest, and responsible way.

Learning to express and resolve feelings appropriately can take years. For addicts whose natural reaction is to hide from feelings and use drugs to numb themselves, becoming aware of feelings can be scary. It's hard to appreciate how a person can become so numb that emotions such as happiness or contentment, or even anger, may not register inside. Addicts have all kinds of emotional garbage that needs to be unloaded in privacy where it is processed and disposed of appropriately.

Often people in recovery will seek relationship advice from within their recovery group. While it is natural for people to seek advice from their peers, it's not always the best thing to do. It certainly doesn't make sense, for example, to seek advice about relationships and expressing feelings from people who have not yet healed those very things.

If you've blocked your feelings for years, you have to deal with the source of what that's about. I recommend that people get personal counseling and participate in relationships and recovery retreats on an ongoing basis. Relationship retreats are an effective way to address the issues that addicts face in learning to communicate and function in a healthy relationship. Learning to express feelings in an open and honest manner takes time and attention—it's like going back to school to learn skills that were not learned in childhood.

The more a person works on healing their emotional wounds, the easier it will be to attract and maintain a long-term, meaningful, love relationship. In recovery, the biggest challenge is to learn to love in a conscious and mature way. If addicts are to find or rebuild, and maintain a long-term, loving relationship, they have to learn to understand and express feelings, and be able to show love and appreciation.

I am someone who has no difficulty telling people I love them. I tell that to my sons almost every time I speak with them. It was not easy for me in my early recovery to be so forthright—it is one of those things that got easier with practice. I believe it is so important that we tell those we love how we feel on a consistent basis, and to be forthright and honest with them.

For me, love is not a *feeling* so much as it is an *action*. We love when we make a conscious choice to support another person on their spiritual journey. But to be able to support someone else, we need to be nurturing our own spiritual growth, which for me is what recovery is about.

INTERDEPENDENT, NOT CODEPENDENT

I've observed, and it's true for me as well, that addicts in relationships tend to be codependents. The term codependency was coined in the 1980s to describe those of us who grew up in dysfunctional homes where we learned certain adaptive behaviors that we carry into adulthood. Children who grow up in homes where it is not okay to talk about problems, where feelings are not openly expressed, and where they dare not rock the boat, have a tendency to attract relationships that are one-sided, emotionally destructive, and abusive.

Codependents, according to the literature, place other people's health, welfare, and safety before their own, and in the process lose contact with their own needs, desires, and sense of self. In response, codependents may try to control everything they can within the relationship.

To have a healthy, mutually satisfying relationship, the goal is to be interdependent, not codependent. An interdependent relationship requires two people to act with integrity, be emotionally stable and not needy, and have established healthy boundaries whereby they clearly communicate what is important and what is not acceptable.

BECOMING EMOTIONALLY AVAILABLE

When I recently asked my first wife Sylvia to describe what I was like in our relationship, she summed it up in two words: emotionally unavailable. I don't think I was any different than the majority of addicts in this respect. As the disease progresses, addicts become more emotionally distant and remote. We are too busy being sick, sad, sorry, tired, or otherwise preoccupied to pay much emotional attention to the ones we love. Our energy, time, and life-force are, for the most part, completely taken up with our drinking or using and everything that goes with it.

Emotionally unavailable people don't, won't, or can't commit to an intimate relationship, despite the fact that deep down that is what they most yearn for. Addicts are very manipulative so they can usually attract a partner when they want. But when the courting stage is over, they go back to their preoccupation with the drug of their choice. In my experience, it is not unusual for addicts to carry on with others outside of a relationship because moral values such as monogamy often get hijacked by the addiction.

When I was with Sylvia, there is no doubt I couldn't commit to spending quality time with her, nor did I try particularly hard to make the relationship work. By the time I was married to Anne, I had done some work on myself and I know I was more responsive to her and her needs within the marriage. But the truth is, I spent much of my time traveling for work during those years, and there is no question this was a way for me to avoid what really needed to be worked on. It was just easier to be away.

Anne and I were each limited in our ability to be emotionally available to one another since we'd both grown up in homes of addiction where unhealthy relationships were modeled. It was not until the collapse of my second marriage that I threw myself into doing some serious counseling to help sort myself out. I did a lot of hard work over a period of several years learning to connect in an intimate way with another person.

I needed to learn to do all the things discussed in previous chapters: to love myself, to forgive, to act with honesty, honor, and integrity within a relationship, to express my innermost feelings, to step away from selfishness, and be empathetic and compassionate. All of this was a process that took time and effort.

I find myself now more at peace in my life than I've ever been. I recently married the most wonderful woman. Jan is a warm, sensitive, and loving person, and for the first time I'm able to fully commit myself to another person, and be more emotionally available than ever before. And, I am still learning...

MOM AND DAD RECONCILED

My parents' reunion is an inspiring illustration of what can be achieved in a relationship where two people love each other despite living through years of chaos. After Dad went to treatment and then relapsed, my mom asked me what she should do regarding her marriage. She had hung in there through 36 years of Dad's addiction, her five children were all grown, and she wanted a more fulfilling life, but because of her evangelical upbringing she felt tremendous angst. I said, "I cannot tell you to leave my dad, but I do know that you have done everything in your power you possibly could. You've been patient and understanding. You've worked at it, and you've prayed. Unfortunately, the person you love is incapable at this point of giving you all the emotional, psychological, spiritual support, and love that is your right as a human being." She left my father and in less than one month he recommitted to his recovery program and quit drinking for good.

Three years later my father, then 61 and living with me, received a letter from Mom which he read to me soon after receiving it. In it she said she had been engaged to a wonderful man, but called the marriage off six days before it was to take place because she still loved my dad. She wanted to know if Dad was open to reconciliation. She told him she was praying for that and she would wait for his reply. You could always tell when Dad was going to cry, his bottom lip would quiver and his left eye would tear up first. He asked me what he should do as he was engaged to a woman in recovery. I told him I couldn't tell him what to do, although inside I was screaming, "Isn't that beautiful!"

His partner understood and released him with love and under-standing. I drove him back to Edmonton where he was reunited with my mother. Mom moved to Vancouver to be with Dad and shortly after they were remarried. Four months later he passed on in Mom's arms in the Frankfurt airport when returning from Germany on their second honeymoon. But what blew me away, and to this day I still marvel at it, is the healing they were able to complete in that short time. In their final four months together they created the most peaceful and loving connection.

CHAPTER NINE

୨୦

RECOVERY AND SPIRITUALITY

Do not struggle. Go with the flow of things, and you will find yourself at one with the mysterious unity of the Universe.

Chung Tzu, 4th century Chinese Philosopher

There is a story in recovery circles about the newcomer who asks a more seasoned member, "What is the spiritual part of this program that everybody talks about?" The fellow replies, "Well, if you can tell me what the other parts are, then maybe I can explain the spiritual part."

The entire process of recovery is a spiritual journey. A spiritual journey does not mean seeking out a specific religion, although for some, religion may well provide the spiritual structure required to successfully work on their recovery. Spirituality is not a stage or a separate part of the experience, nor is it a destination—you don't one day *achieve* spirituality.

Many addicts grew up in family situations where enormous pain caused by abuse or neglect of various kinds left them wounded or spiritually bankrupt. They have a huge void in the center of their being and they try desperately to fill it with substances and/or activities. They don't realize there is nothing missing in them, they just need to get past all of the pain that has been driving them.

Healing this perceived void requires an inward journey which involves attending to the layer upon layer of pain and releasing it. This process starts with surrender—letting go and placing one's trust in a Higher Power. The transformation of the caterpillar to the butterfly is a wonderful analogy for recovery as the caterpillar must surrender to the cocoon before it can become a butterfly. The act of surrender initiates the process allowing addicts to deal with the pain. Every time they encounter pain they need to surrender and let go of their resistance to change. Recovery is a dynamic process. As we grow and change, there are more opportunities created to develop further and evolve one's self. I believe we are never fully finished growing spiritually.

As addicts continue to work on themselves and deal with what the recovery movement calls "defects of character," it is possible to reach a place where they can truly love and trust themselves and others. During their journey of recovery, addicts can find the spiritual nourishment they crave and create a connection with a Higher Power. In fact, I don't know that addicts will ever achieve ongoing, sustained joy, satisfaction, and freedom in their lives, if they do not consciously and consistently focus on their spiritual growth and develop a personal relationship with their Higher Power.

There is a Chinese saying that the longest journey is the journey inward. Spiritual healing is an inward journey that is never finished because we never stop growing ourselves up in life. Spiritual growth is a life-long process.

HP AS A PARTNER

Many people, because of their upbringing and life experiences, do not want to have anything to do with the notion of a Higher Power. I was raised in an Evangelical Southern Baptist Christian setting that taught me about the wrath of God, so I have some appreciation of what it is like for those who want nothing to do with a god of fear and damnation. There are many people, who for their own personal reasons, disdain God, religion, and even spirituality. Some faith groups still see addiction as a sin, not an illness. This adds to the guilt, shame, and remorse the addict already carries. It can also add to the feelings of guilt, shame, and helplessness for family members as well.

Surrendering to a Higher Power does not need to be about turning over one's will and life to a God of any particular religious faith. It may simply be surrendering to the desire to take life in a new direction. No matter what direction we choose, the foundation of this act is surrender of our ego—to get of out of our own way.

Recovery talks about God as being 'Good Orderly Direction,' which for some is a totally new concept. I know I did not have consistent good and orderly direction in my childhood, and definitely not in my teenage and young adult years. If the notion of accepting a Higher Power is too much in the beginning, then I would ask a person not to get too hung up on it. Instead they should let go and trust that life has a way of working out for the best, when we believe that to be the case. By keeping an open mind, and being grateful for everything that comes along, addicts will soon see evidence of something greater at work in their lives, and the idea of a Higher Power at work may not seem so threatening after a while. Some addicts go from having God *no-where* in their lives, to having a God that is *now-here*. [Isn't it wonderful what we can do with words sometimes?]

As people grow in their relationship with a Higher Power, life becomes easier as they learn to let go and trust. I can relate this to when I got to personally know the CEO of the company I worked for during the eighties and nineties. This man was able and willing to do much more for our efforts because of the personal relationship he and I developed. In the same way, God is always willing to help us. Our job is to surrender and ask for help. As our partnership strengthens, we find we *can* address any situation as it comes up. Eventually we become free from our fears and obsessions and truly become happy, joyous, and free.

People conceptualize their understanding of a Higher Power in diverse and different ways. When I moved to BC, my first recovery mentor was Bill, a successful rough-spoken businessman with a heart as big as a Mack truck. He told me his Higher Power was his business partner in the business of daily living. He explained it this way, "I have a business partner I cannot see, but whom I have learned to trust implicitly."

He went on to say that he talks to his business partner every morning without fail saying, "Here is a list of the things I need to handle today. Partner, you know I am too busy to handle all these items here, or too emotional to deal with these other issues right now. I'm not where I need to be and you know that. For this next 24 hours, I am going to give you these items on the list, and my priorities for the day will be these other items. When I'm finished with these, you can give me back what you think I am ready to deal with. I know that as my partner, you will never give me more than I can handle, nor would you bring me this far to let me down."

I can tell you that Bill died a happy and contented man. I often think about him when my life gets too chaotic. Trusting in a Higher Power not only helps alleviate stress, it is an exceedingly empowering way to live. Once people make the decision to change or take action, I believe the Creator will be there to support the change. We will always be guided on the next step of the journey.

There is an anecdote I really appreciate that explains how God works in the physical world. The story is about a man caught in a flash flood. As the waters start to rise, a man on a horse comes to this fellow's house and says, "Quick, come with me." The fellow says, "No, I will wait upon God to save me." As the water gets higher, he climbs to the first floor of the house. Soon another man comes by in a boat and says,

"Quick, get into the boat with me." Again he says, "No, I will wait upon God to save me." The water continues to rise and the man is now clinging to the roof, the final stop before pending doom. A helicopter hovers overhead and the man inside shouts down, "Quick, grab this rope and we will take you to safety." Again, our fellow says, "No, I will wait upon God to save me."

Before long he drowns. When he is in Heaven he asks God, "Why did you not save me in my time of need?" God replies, "Three times I tried to save you. First I sent a man on a horse, then I sent a man in a boat, and finally I sent you a helicopter, but you refused all my help." God works through other people so we may want to be open to those who come into our life. They are not there by sheer coincidence.

ACCEPTING CHANGE

One of the best known quotes or sayings associated with 12-step programs is the Serenity Prayer: "God grant me the serenity to accept the things I cannot change; the courage to change the things I can; and the wisdom to know the difference." This prayer, although not originally written for addicts, certainly speaks directly to all addicts and helps all of us understand the concept of acceptance.

Acceptance goes hand-in-hand with surrender—when we surrender, we accept that we can't do it alone, and when we move into acceptance we surrender ourselves to a higher wisdom that helps us to know the difference between what we cannot change (others) and what we can (ourselves).

A third ingredient for me in this discussion is the virtue of honesty, one of the four key virtues discussed earlier in the book. However, when considering the intertwined role of acceptance and surrender, we also need to appreciate that it requires we be brutally honest with ourselves and others. We have to accept that whatever happened has happened for a reason. When we can do that, the peaceful feeling that comes with it allows us to reach a place where we can surrender and let go.

I like to use acronyms when I can, so I find it remarkable that the acronym for acceptance, surrender, and honesty is A.S.H. For me, this brings to mind ashes, and a visual picture of the phoenix rising from the ashes. Interesting isn't it, that finding recovery for so many of us is akin to the phoenix rising from the ashes…

But back to this concept of acceptance. Addicts in recovery are well advised to accept that sometimes they must let go of those people, places, things, or situations which have kept them in their dysfunctional comfort zone. Change in and of itself is not painful—it is our resistance to change that causes difficulties. If we decide to hang on to certain things for the wrong reasons then, inevitably, the universe will provide the opportunity for change. Should we then resist the change, it's going to be painful. The key is to let go and go with the flow, by putting our trust and faith in a Higher Power.

As we learn to trust and let go of our need to control outcomes, serenity replaces fear, and not only do we find ample courage, we also[1] have a better intuitive sense of what we need to do. It makes sense that as all of the negative clutter in our mind disappears, we become more open and in tune with the higher aspects of life.

Recovery, as with life, is about making choices. Every day we make choices that will either move us forward in our spiritual growth, or cause us to stay stuck. I recently received one of those emails that make the rounds on the Internet providing some worldly wisdom for all who take the time to read it through. It struck me that this particular story (author unknown) beautifully and succinctly describes the impact of our choices. The story is titled "Two Wolves" and goes like this:

One evening, a Cherokee elder told his grandson about a battle that goes on inside people. He said, "My son, the battle is between two 'wolves' inside us all. One is Evil. It is anger, envy, jealousy, sorrow, regret, greed, arrogance, self-pity, guilt, resentment, inferiority, lies, false pride, superiority, and ego. The other is Good. It is joy, peace, love, hope, serenity, humility, kindness, benevolence, empathy, generosity, truth, compassion and faith."

The grandson thought about it for a minute and then asked his grandfather, "Which wolf wins?"

The Cherokee grandfather simply replied, "The one you feed."

As we grow spiritually, we learn that we have a choice about how we respond to what happens—what "wolf we decide to feed."

Recovery circles talk a lot about choices. An analogy I once heard compares the choice addicts have to make at some point to that of jumping off a boat while holding a heavy rock. If addicts want to come back up to the surface, they have to let go of the rock. At some point, recovery is about making a choice to let go of the drug, and trusting that something better replaces it. It is not complex—*drop the rock!*

SPIRITUAL PRINCIPLES

While I am the first to acknowledge that there are people who have found contented recovery without attending a 12-step program, my professional bias is to recommend this route because I have witnessed their success more times than not. Twelve-step recovery programs provide a roadmap for the addict to achieve and maintain recovery. Because of their success, they have been adapted in numerous ways by different organizations around the world.

All 12-step programs make it clear that one's ongoing recovery depends upon one's spiritual condition. There is no question that the steps are spiritual in the sense that they are about doing the inner work that will bring about a healing of body, mind, and spirit.

The importance of developing both values and virtues has been discussed throughout this book. If the 12-steps provide the roadmap for the journey or recovery, then values provide the boundaries. They act like those bumps on the road that let us know when we are straying from our lane. They give order, balance, and meaning to our lives. Once we have determined our personal values, we can organize our life around them. They give us a framework upon which to make decisions and to know how to act with integrity.

Virtues then are the fuel that propel us forward. Developing different virtues allows us to develop our highest and best self. Virtues are

An Act of Surrender

the opposite of our character defects—consciously working on them allows us to achieve and sustain full recovery.

In order to live our values, we must call upon our virtues. For example, if you hold the value that having intimate, loving relationships are most important to you, then you need to call upon such virtues as honesty, faithfulness, forgiveness, compassion, acceptance, and love.

If living your life with integrity is another value you hold, then you might be well advised to work on, and develop, the virtues of trustworthiness, honesty, openness, and gratitude. These might not be the only virtues to work on, but it's a good beginning.

The steps of 12-step recovery programs were converted to what are referred to as the Twelve Principles. For me, these single words or phrases are a combination of virtues and values. They are:

1. Honesty
2. Hope
3. Faith
4. Courage
5. Integrity
6. Willingness
7. Humanity
8. Brotherly/Sisterly love
9. Discipline
10. Perseverance
11. Awareness of God
12. Service

162

I would say that the first 10 of these principles are virtues that we can work on developing and the last two are values that we might organize our life around.

SPIRITUAL DISCIPLINES

The development of daily spiritual practices or disciplines greatly enhance a person's development. While there are many different forms these practices may take, four that I have incorporated into my life are prayer, meditation, having a spiritual advisor, and rituals.

I have conversations with God every day. That is what prayer and meditation are all about for me. Sometimes I kneel and talk out loud, other times I talk silently in my head as I'm driving somewhere, or doing the usual routine things in my life. When I kneel to pray, I see that as humbling myself before my Creator. True humility involves knowing where your power comes from and what the Creator is doing for you. Asking God for help is not about being weak, but about being strong enough to acknowledge and be grateful for the presence of a Higher Power in our life. The value in having a time of sacred communion with God cannot be overstated.

In 2007, I had the good fortune to go on a Caribbean cruise with a good friend, Bob. Bob was into his second year of recovery when he was diagnosed with pancreatic and liver cancer. Sadly, less than six months later, Bob passed on. During the trip, I would openly pray with Bob, as I am very comfortable doing so. A few days before we flew home, I asked Bob if he would like to share a prayer with me. He agreed and then proceeded to ask God to give love and support to all his family members.

When he was done I said to him, "Bob, you didn't ask for anything for yourself."

With a look of total surprise, and tears in his eyes, he asked, "Can I do that?"

I said, "Of course, you have an illness. You can ask for God's help."

Many of us are raised with the misconception that it is selfish and not right to ask God to help us out, especially in a time of need. I know now that this is anything but the truth. The Universe, the Creator, God, whatever word you chose to use, exists to carry out our wishes. God wants us to ask for help, no matter how small or how large the request may be. Now we might not always get what we ask for, but we will always get what is best when we look at the bigger picture of our lives. It may take some time for us to see that, and what we get may be hard to accept sometimes, but life always works out, and God's support and love are always there for us.

I believe that heartfelt, intense, focused prayer will result in miracles. A number of years ago I was away on business when I got a call that my youngest son was having some difficult life challenges. I got down on my knees in my hotel room and, choked with emotion, asked God to help my son. A few minutes into my prayer I experienced a sensation like warm, heavy milk being poured over me. I can only relate it to what the Bible calls "the anointing of the holy spirit."

In that moment a voice in my head told me that no matter what happened in my son's life, God would protect him and keep him safe. It doesn't surprise me that my Higher Power would communicate with me, but it certainly fills me with awe. Since then, when I feel anxious for my son, I remind myself of God's promise and I'm able to relax.

It may seem silly or naïve, but expressing our feelings to God and asking for help, for any reason whatsoever, can be very powerful. It is also important to express our gratitude for what is good in our life, even if we feel there's not much to be thankful for at the time.

If you are new to prayer, then keep it short and simple and let the practice build as you get more comfortable. Once you've asked God for something for yourself or for someone else, express thanks, then relax knowing you have done your part, and leave it in the hands of the Creator. Be patient and allow things to unfold gracefully, trusting that divine energy is at work. Placing our trust in God eliminates worry, fear, and the continual obsessing addicts are prone to do. I've always appreciated the saying: "If you pray why worry; if you worry why pray." To improve your spiritual contact with God, I recommend making it a point to stop and talk with God for a few minutes in your mind at perhaps half a dozen established times during the day.

The practice of meditation can also have tremendous value on several different levels for those in recovery. Sitting quietly and focusing on one's breathing is a way to relax and let go of the daily stresses of life. Therapists will recommend meditation as a tool for observing our thoughts and feelings as they occur in the present moment. This allows us to become more conscious of where we are, and where we may need to change. Meditation is also described as a spiritual practice where the mind can transcend its preoccupation with day-to-day concerns and experience a sense of connectedness with a higher consciousness.

Some people say that prayer is talking to God, and meditation is listening to God. For those who make it a regular practice, research has shown prayer and meditation to be effective ways to improve one's quality of life and sense of purpose. In fact, step 11 of 12-step programs puts it perfectly when it describes prayer and meditation as the means "to improve our conscious contact with God *as we understood Him.*"

The writers of the 12-step program understood that addicts have such ego issues that they would find it difficult, if not impossible, to willingly surrender themselves to a Higher Power. They knew, however, that it was critical to make conscious contact with a Higher Power for recovery to begin, and continue to deepen as people move forward in their willingness to handle life's circumstances in a responsible, accountable way. This is why 12-step programs advise addicts to work with a spiritual advisor, in addition to having a mentor or sponsor.

For more than 30 years I've had Pastor Virgil Olson and Elder Norm Botterill as my spiritual advisors. Through good times and bad, I would sit with either one of these deeply spiritual men and tell them all that was in my heart. Both have a beautiful way of receiving what I have to say, and it always helps me to heal. The recovery program says an addict needs to improve his or her conscious contact with God, and often a person of faith is just the one to help. I am so grateful that I have these two spiritual advisors in my life and for all that they have taught me, especially around the concept of forgiveness.

The fourth spiritual practice I believe in is ritual. It is my experience that rituals can affect the energy of a room in a tangible way and bring about a calm and peaceful feeling. It can be something as simple as lighting candles before sitting down to meditate. With all recovery groups there are certain 'ritualistic' ways of starting and moving through meetings, just as the same is true of any faith service. I am often aware of healing energy in a recovery meeting. I remember going to meetings early in my recovery and I'd be suffering from a stress headache and stiff neck. As I sat in the energy of the room and moved through the different rituals, I soon began to feel better.

SPIRITUAL AWAKENINGS

Recovery programs will often talk about the possibility of having a spiritual awakening. This experience is different for everyone, but for many people it is a gradual process that happens incrementally as they learn to place their trust in God. For others, a spiritual awakening can be a profound experience that may include some kind of epiphany or deep insight into their life.

I had a spiritual awakening experience around the third month of my recovery when driving by myself to our cabin on Lake Athabasca, north of Edmonton. This was not long after my experience of the 'penny dropping' and I knew without doubt I was an addict. As I drove along the highway, I could see that farmers had recently mowed the hay that grows in the ditches. Alongside this particular stretch of road, wild clover had been cut in the past few hours and was still lying there. I suddenly got a waft of the aroma. Anyone from the prairies will know the smell I speak of—it is divine. I felt compelled to pull the car over and get out.

I sat on the fender of the car and just took in the smell and the sights of the countryside. As I did, I felt that I was one with all of creation and with God. My life took on a whole new sense of peace and acceptance, and I knew in that moment, from the depth of my soul, that my Higher Power was guiding and taking care of me. The message was very clear—I was going to be okay despite myself. I cried with relief and happiness as I absorbed this reality into my being.

In one sense, you could say that there was nothing particularly special about stopping to enjoy the sights and smells of the countryside. What made this moment extraordinary for me was the realization that we are not separate, but one with God, a Higher Power that will protect us if we just allow it to be. I always thought it was interesting that events in my life had conspired to have me be in that place at that time, to have that experience.

As a final thought on spirituality, I just want to say to those who are just consciously starting a spiritual journey that the rewards you will receive are beyond measure. I believe that when we ask God into our lives, we are showered with gifts—the gifts of loving relationships, peace and happiness, and continued contentment. It's important to know, however, that as you receive these gifts in your life, you need to pass them on to others. Through this process of giving and receiving, we grow closer to becoming our authentic self.

CHAPTER TEN

ॐ

ADDICTION, RECOVERY, AND FAMILIES

Accept the things to which fate binds you, and love the people with whom fate brings you together, but do so with all your heart.

Marcus Aurelius, 121-180, Roman Emperor

I grew up in a loving and caring, but chronically dysfunctional family. While I've had people argue that such is impossible, that the two cannot co-exist, it was true for my family and for many other families I've worked with. My mother is a kind, compassionate person and she dearly loved my father. Because of this she innocently went to great lengths to cover-up and compensate for his alcoholism and the chaos that it created.

On many occasions my dad would pass out on the couch, sometimes falling forward hitting the rug. Mom would find him and get him back onto the couch or the bed if she could. She did this because she loved him and she wanted to hide what was going on from us kids. But she also thought she was part of the problem, because my dad, like most addicts, would blame her for his problems.

The family was always under stress, but it was never acknowledged. My family, as other families do, adjusted to the situation in predictable ways.

When my mother married my father, she had no experience whatsoever with addiction. Nor did she have a real understanding of how a healthy relationship between a husband and wife should look. Her own father died when she was young and she grew up in a place where addiction was not seen. In fact, in her upbringing the very presence of it was an outright sin against God. She did not understand that compulsive drinking was an addiction, that addiction was an illness, and that the illness was treatable. All she could do was pray it would go away so her children did not have to grow up in it, and that the man she loved would change. She did everything possible to keep it secret, act as though it wasn't a problem, and attempt to make up for my father's short-comings. Addiction literature calls this "enabling."

My mother's story is not unique. Even today, when so much more is known about addiction, families live in homes where the addiction is not acknowledged. In these homes denial and cover-up are so embedded in the family culture and way of doing things that family members don't realize what they're doing. I've worked with families of great wealth who on the exterior appeared enormously successful, but on the inside were desperately dysfunctional. The sad part is, it doesn't have to be this way.

Studies show that a large percentage of women raised in a home with an alcoholic father attract men who are, or become, addicts. Where we have a woman with an alcoholic father raised in a dysfunctional home, marrying an alcoholic, there is little chance their children will know what a healthy relationship looks like. Even if the drinking or using stops, it isn't likely these parents know how to model effective ways to resolve conflict, deal with pain, or even demonstrate love, compassion, acceptance, intimacy, etcetera. The cycle continues when these children get into relationships—it is truly generational. They don't talk about their feelings, they tolerate deception or lies, and they work to keep the peace at all costs. It's a recipe for failure that will take time and effort to change through learning new behaviors. Effective, empowered relationships *are* possible and can be developed with a conscientious effort.

RAISING THE BOTTOM

Without education and knowledge, family members usually don't realize that their actions do not help, but instead result in supporting the addict's behavior. Despite the best of intentions, families minimize situations by allowing addicts to avoid taking responsibility, or even comprehending that they are responsible for their own actions, and so the addiction continues to worsen with seemingly little or no consequences. For addicts, who are masterful manipulators, enabling behaviors play right into their hands.

I have worked with families who were so entrenched in denial that they refused to accept the seriousness of their situation. As family members move deeper into denial, they start feeling anger, guilt, remorse, and self-pity, often without realizing the source of their upset. They lose the ability to see reality and to deal with problems appropriately. It often takes some kind of crisis for families to wake up and realize what they've been doing. Families often do whatever they can to protect the addict, desperately hoping things will change if the addict just knew how much he or she were loved. Some families live in fear of anger or violence being directed at them, so they don't rock the boat. There are many different reasons why families adopt enabling behaviors to cope with the situations they live in day after day.

Families can play an extremely vital role in 'raising the bottom' for addicts, helping them to reach a place where they agree they need help. Family members can do this by learning about addiction and ending their enabling behaviors. Addicts generally will not hit bottom or realize they need to stop their destructive behavior until they experience a sense of loss, or fear that they are going to lose something they value. This could be their family, friends, work, status, health, or freedom. When family and friends stop enabling, addicts will usually start to realize that they need to change.

My experience is that when a family also does the same six things as addicts (as described in Chapter Six), the likelihood their loved one will grab onto and maintain recovery is dramatically increased. However, I have worked with many family members who agree to the six stipulations but don't maintain their commitment over the longer term. Addicts can get clean and sober without their families' help, but it's a whole lot easier for everyone if family members know how to be supportive. Sometimes families assume their loved ones are doing well in recovery, so they pull back from both caring for themselves and providing support. Or, their loved one relapses and they simply give up hope and stop participating in their own prescribed recovery process.

We are talking about one of the most devastating and terminal illnesses today, a disease that pulls everybody close to them down. When family members tell me it's not *their* problem, or that they don't have the time to go to a support group meeting once a week, it hurts my heart every time.

Unfortunately, many families have a tendency to relapse and fall back into old patterns of behavior. In large part this is because they fail to fully appreciate that addiction is an disease, and that for recovery to be sustained, it must involve the transformation of the whole family. Families must keep in mind that their own recovery, and that of their addicted loved one, need to be managed on an ongoing basis in order to establish a new way of being.

BABY ELEPHANTS

I attended a retreat where the guest speaker shared a wonderful analogy for growing up in a home with addiction or other abuses. He described how baby elephants in India are trained to not wander off. When an elephant is young, one end of a rope is tied to its hind leg and the other end to a sturdy tree. When the elephant reaches the length of the rope it tries desperately to pull free, walking back and forth, yanking at the rope over and over again. Finally, with tears in its eyes, the little elephant simply gives up trying. From that point on, the trainer just needs to tie the rope to a small stake in the ground, and when the elephant feels the rope tug on its leg, it stays there just within the length of the tug. The fully grown elephant doesn't realize it does not have to be this way, that with an easy pull it would be free.

The speaker said, "Those are baby elephant learnings and in the same way, messages become ingrained in us as children which no longer have any relevance for us as adults. These baby elephant learnings act as blocks or barriers, and they can unconsciously impact the decisions we make in our adult life."

Children learn early to cope by developing defenses to accommodate the addicted adult. These defense systems become ingrained in their personalities, so that as adults they react to situations the same way they did as children. A couple of classic examples of defense mechanisms are the need to please everyone all of the time, and the inability to make a definitive decision for fear of making the wrong one. Unfortunately, these behaviors aren't appropriate or productive.

The value of in-depth therapy, both individual personal counseling and participating at a residential treatment center, is that it is possible to start to identify baby elephant learnings and change them. Most often, family members are not aware of the degree to which they have been impacted, especially if they have lived with dysfunction for some time.

Family programs talk about three "C's"—you didn't Cause it, you can't Control it, and you can't Cure it. A family program is designed to help family members identify and heal their own emotional wounds, and to learn to live a meaningful life regardless of what the addict does. Adults, who may have suffered as a result of growing up with an emotionally absent and/or abusive parents, or who have had an abusive partner, would benefit enormously from this type of specialized therapy, even if that person in their life left or died years earlier.

Another reason for family treatment is that quite often the spouse or partner of an addict is codependent because he or she grew up in a dysfunctional home. These partners likely also developed codependent behaviors if they lived under siege of active addiction for some time. If these partners do not do any work on healing themselves, when the addict cleans up, the family frequently falls apart. Partners end up leaving because they are programmed to live in a chaotic environment—it is familiar territory, a dysfunctional comfort zone for them. These partners no longer know how to relate to this other person who has been changed by treatment and is now actively pursuing recovery. Again, I cannot stress enough the value of the partner or spouse doing what they need to do to heal their own wounds. In relationships we are never stagnant for long, we are always growing—if not together, then we're growing apart.

RAISING KIDS TODAY

As a father of two boys now in their twenties, and as a professional working in the addictions field for over 30 years, I've seen what goes on with young people and alcohol and drugs. There is no question that kids are experimenting with drugs at a much younger age, with the first time use sometimes being age 10 to 12, and in some cases kids as young as eight and nine are exposed to drugs. Even more frightening is the undisputed fact that the potency and variety of drugs they are experimenting with is much greater than 10 or 20 years ago.

When I work with families who have a teenager or young adult in trouble, it is not difficult to quickly determine which ones hold a greater chance for success. The more stable the family—the more capable they are of treating their child with love, respect, honor, and a willingness to hold their child accountable—the greater the likelihood their child will grab onto recovery and sustain it. It is a harder grab at the other end of the spectrum when a family operates under a high level of chaos and disconnection, and under its own cloud of addiction or denial disorders.

Just as the more things change, the more they stay the same, the favorite drug of kids today is the same as their parents' favorite drug: alcohol. Despite all of the media attention given to street drugs, such as crystal meth and cocaine, the fact is that alcohol is still, by far, the greatest concern. Researchers are finding that the younger people are when they start drinking, the greater the likelihood of becoming addicted.

Research has shown that areas of a teenager's brain, including the area that controls impulsive behavior, are still developing, so rewiring of the brain happens much more quickly. There are parents who give their kids marijuana because the parents smoke it at home and want to be open and honest. They share their belief that using marijuana is much less harmful than alcohol, and not as likely to result in any form of legal issues such as impaired driving or public intoxication. I have only one thing to say to these people: marijuana is not a harmless drug—giving it to kids is simply asking for trouble because its potency is so strong and it can be addictive.

If parents suspect their child is using drugs they need to get professional advice. I have had to coach many parents to take a tough love approach and change the locks on their homes, put jewelry in safe places, and make sure they don't leave cash lying around. If their child agrees to go for counseling or treatment, then the parents would be well advised to get professional help in finding appropriate care. Adolescents require specialized treatment by people who know how to work with young people.

Parents who are actively involved in their kids' lives can have a very powerful influence on an adolescent's drug use. There is also good research showing that teaching values and spiritual principles can reduce the likelihood that young people will start using drugs early, and may prevent them from developing a more serious problem. Young people will also grab onto recovery more quickly if they were raised with a strong set of spiritual values. They won't struggle with the concept of a Higher Power, or the need to surrender and reach out for help.

When a child gets into serious trouble with drugs and gets help, it is important that the family takes the time to fully understand the nature of this disease. I have seen situations where the child comes home from treatment to a loving, supportive family where expectations are high and there is an unspoken current of tension. The young addict relapses under pressure, and the family, often the father, becomes more anxious and erupts in anger. This kind of response justifies for addicts why they need to drink or use. In fact, research shows that generally there is a greater chance of relapse for young addicts who, after treatment, go back to live with parents who have not participated in a solid educational program where they can learn about their own role in addiction and recovery.

I strongly urge parents to participate in an intensive supportive family program, as well as attend regular family support meetings. In family programs parents learn about the disease of addiction, and just as important, they can learn about their own issues. Family programs allow the whole family to understand and address their enabling behaviors. Attending support meetings will let them know their situation is not unique, that others have dealt with and come through similar experiences.

My advice to parents today is to begin to talk openly and honestly about drugs when the children are young and not just leave this up to the schools. My colleagues and I have organized a number of community awareness sessions called "Is 13 Too Late?" The premise is that age 13 is in fact much too late to begin a conversation about drugs in today's society. Anne and I started talking about drugs and alcohol with our sons when they were eight or nine. We also stressed the fact that addiction runs in both sides of our family, just like heart disease runs in families, and that they would need to handle it like any kind of genetic family illness. I brought videos about addiction home from work and we watched them as a family and talked about them together.

As the boys got older and started drinking, my approach was always to be reasonable, respectful, and fair, and to encourage them to be open and honest with me. I talked with them about the fact that life is about choices. They can say yes to something, or they can say no, and in either case there will be consequences. When something bad happens in their life, they always have a choice as to how they respond to it—they can accept what happened, learn from it and make the most of it, or they can stay stuck in resistance and resentment. It's about choices and consequences.

LIFE COMES FULL CIRCLE

As life would have it, while I first began working on this section of this book, my youngest son Rob entered into treatment for cocaine, alcohol, and marijuana addiction. Even with everything we did to prepare both our boys, one of them did succumb to addiction. I got to learn first-hand how difficult the advice I give to other families with an addict can really be: *The more you love, the closer you are, the more you see, the more it hurts, the less capable you are of changing that person—love them, learn about the addiction, and get out of the way!*

I believe I did a lot of things wrong, for all the right reasons with my son. I discovered it is far easier for me to give guidance and to work with someone else's child than my own. I did what most parents do, I enabled. I knew Rob had been drinking and using marijuana for several years. It was only when he told me he was ready to go to treatment (at the age of 25, the same age I was when I stopped) that he admitted he had a cocaine problem.

Over the years, there were a few incidents—addicts tend to get into trouble. One such time occurred when Rob was 19. I was awakened from a deep sleep by an police officer knocking on the door of my home. She wanted to know if this is where my son lived. My heart pounding I responded yes and asked what was wrong. She said his vehicle had been involved in a single vehicle accident. I asked if he was okay, and she replied she didn't know. Apparently someone saw his car drive straight through a T-intersection, through a creek bed and into the brush on the other side. The driver got out of the car and fled into a nearby heavily wooded park.

I flashed back to when I had my accident near Lestock when, if it had not been for my friend seeing me running into the field, I would have bled to death. I asked the officer what state the interior of the car was in and she said there were lots of beer cans.

I pleaded, "Do you know if there was blood? Was the front window smashed in? Was the steering wheel damaged?" I needed to know if Rob might be bleeding to death. She said the inside of the vehicle had no such indications. After she left I sat on the front steps of the house crying and praying, asking God to keep my son safe from harm, just as my mother had done so many times for me.

Ten minutes later he stumbled up the backstairs quite drunk and obviously shaken. He said, "Dad, I had an accident" and I replied, "I know you did." I looked him over to see there were no bruises or cuts and simply said "Let's go to bed, we'll deal with this tomorrow." I thank

God to this day that no one was killed or injured and no public damage had been done.

When we went to the scene the next day it was obvious only a miracle prevented a much more serious crash. It was truly by the grace of God that Rob had not been seriously injured or killed. We then visited the police office; he was not charged or fined, as no one was hurt, there was no public or private property damage, and he was not at the scene to be tested for alcohol.

Rob had other run-ins with the law, a number of vehicle accidents, road-side suspensions, and an impaired driving conviction. I now look back and ask myself, could I have, or should I have intervened sooner? Yes, we'd had many talks about addiction, but I never wanted to be too heavy-handed with him. He did go for counseling a few times and Anne and I talked about doing an intervention, but we never did.

I made the conscious choice to see my son as an adult who should be able to exercise a certain amount of control. He knew there was to be no drunkenness or use of illegal drugs on our property. In hindsight, I perhaps should have done things differently. I did not take the tough love approach at first that I often counsel other parents to take. There is no question that the closer you are to someone in trouble, the more it hurts, and the less likely you are to do all the right things—unless you have a lot of sound outside guidance.

LIFE COMES FULL CIRCLE AGAIN

Despite the fact my boys have never seen me drunk or on drugs, one of my sons developed a chemical dependency. When children are genetically predisposed and grow up witnessing active addiction, it just compounds the likelihood they are going to get into difficulties. Such was the case for my niece Ashley, Cheri's only daughter.

There is no question Ashley's childhood was difficult. When she came along, Cheri chose the birth of that child as a single mother, although she did not have the support of the father. Growing up, Ashley had little contact with her father. Her mother was often in active addiction, and some of her partners were also active addicts. Cheri didn't attract the healthiest of relationships. So Ashley's life was not easy, although she was loved. I learned later from Ashley that she started using alcohol at the age of 13. When Cheri died, Ashley was 17, and understandably, things got even more difficult. One can only imagine the feelings of loss and abandonment, the anxiety and desperation she must have been feeling. My family tried as best we could to do something, but Ashley would not admit to needing help.

On February 19, 2006, at the age of 27, Ashley collapsed in her bathroom and was rushed to hospital. The staff had no idea that they were dealing with a late stage alcoholic, they just knew they had a very sick young woman on their hands. It was four days before the hospital found my mother's number and she could tell the staff that Ashley had a history of alcohol abuse. Ashley had been living for some time predominantly on vodka, and few other fluids or food, so her physical health was grave. She went into DT's or delirium tremens which can result in death. Twice during the first 10 days of her hospital stay she almost died. Fortunately, good medical care and the prayers of many, especially my mom's, saved her.

My brother, my mother, Ashley's brother and his father, Ashley's boyfriend, Dr. Graham, the addictions specialist, and I undertook an intervention in the hospital room as soon as she was well enough. Ashley had watched those intervention programs on television, so she knew something was up. Sometimes, in the midst of her drinking, she would say to my mom or me, "Why does no one do an intervention on me?" We had discussed it but knew she wasn't ready. With this intervention, she agreed to go to treatment, but she was not physically, emotionally, or mentally capable of handling intensive residential care just yet.

Ashley agreed to come and live in my home for two months, and my 86-year-old mother helped provide support. It had its trying moments for all of us, but with love and understanding, Ashley's body and spirit began the healing process. When she had been in the hospital, I thought she looked to be at least twice her age. But the body's ability to heal and rebuild itself is amazing. With those months of care and rest, she transformed back to a beautiful young woman. During this time, she connected with a good addictions counselor. She had three months of being clean and sober before entering residential treatment for two months.

Ironically, Ashley's recovery date is the same as mine, February 19. Ashley has been clean and sober for more than three years now. Given where she started, she has come a long way...a true miracle indeed.

CHAPTER ELEVEN

℘

ADDICTION, RECOVERY, AND THE WORKPLACE

Truth is the only safe ground to stand on.

Elizabeth Cady Stanton, 1815-1902, American Social Activist

In the early 1980s, I received a call from one of my employer's lawyers telling me that an hourly employee who worked and lived in one of the remote logging camps was found to be in possession of marijuana on company property. The lawyer wondered what my thoughts were on bringing in the police dogs to search the premises, as company officials did not believe this was an isolated incident.

I said, "If you do that, then you need to run the dogs through the homes of management people on the same company property, as well as those of hourly workers." I had had a lot of experience at that logging camp and suspected that, percentage-wise, there were just as many management personnel as hourly people smoking dope, and I felt strongly that everyone should be treated equally. In the end, the company decided not to do anything—they didn't want the possibility of management people being arrested on company property.

Over the years I heard about a number of fatalities involving loggers who had toked up before going off to work. Co-workers and supervisors would know this was the case, but no one did anything. It is amazing to me that generally reliable people allow co-workers to do their job while under the influence of drugs or alcohol. Lives are lost because workers think that if someone is impaired on the job (smoking a joint, suffering from a hangover), it is none of their business. They are afraid of the repercussions. Co-workers cover-up or do the work for a buddy because they don't want to be seen as rats. Or, because they themselves may be in the same situation some time, they look after each other.

I recall one incident where a fellow talked to a supervisor about a co-worker's drug use and a few days later someone put a bottle of rat poison in the fellow's lunch box. This person should have been regarded as a hero for having the courage to care and take action. It is unbelievable that anyone would allow a person to work stoned or even hung-over, let alone ostracize someone for speaking up!

Workplaces can be just as much a player in an addict's life as the family—sometimes this is the only family that person has. Many addicts will do whatever they possibly can to hang on to their jobs. The family may be long gone, but addicts know that it is the job that pays for their drugs. As long as addicts remain employed, employers and unions are in an ideal position to reach out and help.

DRUGS IN THE WORKPLACE

When it comes to drugs in the workplace, alcohol is not the problem it was 20 or 30 years ago. Today, however, there is a considerable amount of cocaine and amphetamines being used by workers, and heroin is on the increase. But the drug most commonly being used in industrial settings is marijuana.

Marijuana is definitely a drug I would not want to find used at work because of how it affects the user. There is a general feeling in society today that it is a relatively benign drug, but THC, the active ingredient in marijuana is much more powerful than in the past. Unquestionably, marijuana is a dangerous drug because it impairs coordination and balance, and slows reflexes and reaction time. It also makes it difficult for the user to complete complex tasks, particularly those involving calculations or problem solving, as well as operating moving equipment or machinery.

Another growing concern for the workplace is prescription drugs. Many prescription drugs are more readily available on the street than from a doctor. And who knows what other chemicals are mixed with these street drugs! In any event, a drug is a drug, and drug behavior is drug behavior. It is immaterial whether it is a legal drug or an illegal drug. Someone can get just as stoned on prescription drugs and over-the-counter drugs, and employers, unions, and professional associations all need to pay attention.

THE ENABLING WORKPLACE

One of the biggest challenges in the workplace is the favoritism that managers and union leaders practice, without understanding the consequences. The more workers are liked, or the longer they have been working there, the more they will get away with because of the enabling that goes on, and the greater the chances they will be left alone in their addiction. For the drinker/user who has been able to maintain some control, receiving a buy-out package and early retirement removes one of the key restraints that may have acted to slow the progression of the addiction. In many cases these people die within 24 months of alcohol or drug related causes. I have seen far too many cases like this over my career.

On the other hand, relatively new hires in the workplace will get the kind of help that all addicts should get. Chances are that management, with the agreement of the union, is going to offer them professional help if they are unable to perform safely—or they'll be let go.

Workplaces often have the best of intentions to help the employee with an addiction. But good intentions, while understandable and honorable, can be counter-productive and even dangerous. Co-workers might, for example, do things such as ignore the little signs that suggest an employee may be having trouble. They might cover-up for an employee who is late for work or absent because of alcohol or drug use, or find reasons not to follow through with consequences when the person's behavior does not improve.

These enabling behaviors are deeply rooted in the culture of an organization. Frequently there is an unspoken code that if alcohol or drugs are involved in an accident, no one speaks up. We refer to this as a "conspiracy of silence." When the corporate culture gets to this point, ensuring successful interventions requires that the entire workplace structure be viewed as part of the problem. In order to create an environment where a solution is likely to occur, the culture must be addressed. For those who do go to treatment, it is nearly impossible to maintain recovery if they go back to a work setting where drugs are being sold or used.

When enabling systems in the workplace are not addressed, the results are poor attitudes and morale, increased accidents, lowered productivity, strained labor relations, and a reluctance to admit there are problems. The training that my colleagues and I do is all about addressing the workplace enabling that is carried on by everyone all the way down the line, including senior management, managers, supervisors, union leaders, union representatives, and co-workers.

Training helps people become aware of their enabling behaviors and learn how to effectively deal with alcohol and drug problems on the job. Participants learn that when they keep a substance abuser afloat, they are literally sending that person to an earlier grave, and possibly endangering other workers on the job. When managers and workers learn to be accountable and address drug and alcohol concerns, they can put an end to the merry-go-round of denial that goes on. We tell participants that no matter who they are in the organization, they must be responsible for maintaining a healthy, safe work environment by dealing with substance abuse when they are aware of it. Work environments become healthier, with significant increases in morale and productivity, when the crutches are removed and workers stop putting energy into cover-up and denial.

ROLE OF THE EMPLOYER

Some years ago I read that a survey taken in the U.S. concluded that America did not have a problem of job absenteeism and low productivity, but that it had an alcohol and drug problem. I suspect they are right—that a significant percentage of workers are using some sort of mood-altering substance before going to work or during the work day.

Fortunately, some employers are realizing they have to take action because of sky-rocketing costs. There is no question that substance abuse results in absenteeism, accidents, employee turnover, property damage, theft, and increased costs for health benefits. And then on top of that there is a loss of productivity caused by employees' lack of attention to their jobs and muddled thinking when important decisions must be made, and poor morale that prevails when other people must do the substance abuser's work.

Many workplaces are implementing drug testing programs for due diligence so that they can claim they have a program of some kind in place. Unfortunately, drug testing as a prevention strategy, without any accompanying educational programs, does nothing to address enabling, and results in even greater labor relations problems and more cover-ups.

Generally, it is up to managers and supervisors to take corrective action when there is a problem. However, they can sometimes be reluctant to do anything because they don't understand substance abuse issues, nor do they feel adequately qualified to deal with them. In many cases, supervisors have been promoted from the hourly ranks and are often friends with some of the people they now supervise. It can be difficult for them to address a possible substance abuse issue with someone they drank and fished with last weekend and whose family they know well. The resulting inaction ensures that addiction becomes a worse problem as job performance further declines.

Work organizations need to provide a jointly implemented educational strategy about addiction for all workplace leaders, as part of an overall plan. The plan must also include a solid benefits package to provide financial support for continuing care for employees who receive treatment for addiction. Most benefit programs today do not adequately meet the needs of chemical dependency. Financial benefits should also be available to help family members. In addition, there needs to be a continuing care agreement in place when someone returns to work after treatment.

ROLE OF THE UNION

As my dad's drinking intensified, it got to be that drinking didn't interfere with his work so much as work interfered with his drinking. Dad would consistently be tardy or call in sick, and his employers, quite rightfully, went after him. There was one year he held 10 different jobs because he was a good mechanic and could always get hired. He also caused accidents, on and off the job.

One time, in a hangover state, he ran a crane with the boom up across the yard and clipped a power line. When the company came after him, he went to the union which inevitably did what unions traditionally do—work to protect the worker's job at all costs. Many times, the union would be trying hard to save Dad's job, while he would be down at the Army and Navy Club or the Legion drinking. In the meantime, his family was barely surviving. The company and union argued about his job security and income—money that never made it home to my family anyway, and nothing was ever said about his drinking and the consequences to his health, his safety, or the safety of his co-workers. Definitely, no consideration was given by either party to the despair and plight of his family.

In a unionized workplace, addicts generally get away with unproductive and unsafe behaviors longer because of the cover-up, enabling, and denial behaviors that are played out by the union in the name of job protection and job security. Intervention, if it happens, comes at a very late stage as part of a disciplinary action. What is needed is a joint strategy with a goal of much earlier interventions.

Labor needs to have information and knowledge to take a position of accountability. They need to step out of the adversarial arena when it comes to dealing with workers who are experiencing personal troubles. Unions are also employers, sometimes quite large employers, so they can appreciate the need for policies and procedures to deal with substance abuse and addiction issues which can be applied consistently throughout an organization.

On several occasions I heard the director of a rehabilitation program for a large American union speak at substance abuse conferences. He would ask, "Brothers and Sisters, can you tell me in one word what it is we as a union provide to our membership?" The answer from the audience would always be, "protection," to which he would say, "The purpose of all unions is to provide service—unions are service organizations. Our role is to protect all members, but unions should not be protecting one worker at the expense of co-workers, or his or her family. That is a disservice."

REASONABLE, RESPECTFUL, AND FAIR

Twenty-five years ago I worked closely with management and union leaders to implement an Employee Assistance Program (EAP) in a pulp and paper mill. In those days, there was enormous skepticism and fear that the program was just a way to get rid of the people management didn't like. Not long after the EAP was established, two employees were caught in the mill site buying marijuana from another employee. A senior manager called me about the incident and argued that we needed to make an example of this by firing all three of them so it did not happen again. I said to him, "Remember that whatever you do, you'll be setting an example. The question is, what is the example you want to set?"

I then asked, "If this had been whiskey that was exchanging hands, would you be so anxious to fire them all? After all a drug is a drug is a drug. Do you just want to fire them because it is an illegal drug?" When he asked me what I would do, I said, "Suspend them all without pay. Do your fact-finding, and then make your recommendations based on what is reasonable, respectful, and fair."

Of course, the question that was hanging over all of our heads was, would the union grieve it? Fortunately, they were willing to hang tight and wait for the process to unfold.

In the end, the three employees all lost 90 days of wages, which was a much bigger financial cost than if they had gone to court and paid a fine for possession of marijuana. The three agreed to go for a complete assessment for addiction. Two of the three were found to be chemically dependent and they participated in a residential treatment program. Each of them eventually returned to work.

All of the workers at the mill knew the whole story of what had happened and saw how it was handled. The example set by this incident was huge, and as a result the newly implemented Employee Assistance Program definitely gained credibility. Some opponents had originally called it the Employee *Assassination* Program, but this incident proved otherwise.

About a year later, I was at the mill to do training for the EAP committee. A fellow came up to me and introduced himself, saying, "You don't know me but I know you. I am one of the guys caught buying marijuana last year and I ended up going to treatment. It is the best thing that has ever happened to me. My life has been turned around and I've been clean and sober for a year. Just recently I got engaged and now my fiancée and I are buying a house together. Not only that, my union has chosen me to be on the EAP committee." Needless to say, it was a very gratifying moment for me.

FAMILY AND THE WORKPLACE

When facilitating workplace training sessions, I frequently ask participants how many of them grew up in a home where there was a family member who had a substance abuse problem. Usually, about one-half to two-thirds of the participants raise their hands. When I ask how many grew up in a home where there was a psychiatric or mental health issue, it is almost the same percentage. (Some of those may be the same individuals.) I then ask if they would have sought out help if they had known there was assistance available through a family member's workplace. Again, a significant number will raise their hands.

If we can educate families, it will greatly increase our ability to assist workers. That's why, in 1981, we worked diligently to ensure that families were included in the Employee Assistance Program. In 1988 the joint program was renamed the Employee *and Family* Assistance Program (EFAP)—the unions and the company were one of the first I know of to do this. Families need to know that the workplace will support them in helping their loved ones. Now many interventions are done where family members, co-workers, union reps, and supervisors are all present, or directly involved in some way.

A good example of the need to provide coverage for family members is a case where a teenager, the daughter of a male employee, became concerned about the anger she witnessed between her parents. She contacted the EFAP counseling office, and after a couple of sessions convinced her mother to go for counseling. It became evident that the girl's father had a problem with addiction. He ended up seeing the counselor and then going to residential treatment. Here was a teenager who saved her family, and also potentially saved both the company and the union unnecessary conflict and considerable dollars.

Something else that workplaces generally do not understand is the impact an addicted family member can have on an employee, and thus on the work environment. When workers are constantly worried about their spouse, or one of their children, they will understandably let their mind wander while trying to do their job. This can be as much of an impairment to doing their job safely as if they had come to work stoned or hung-over.

I worked with a fellow whose wife had left him with four daughters to raise on his own. His 15-year-old daughter got involved with drugs and eventually ended up being enticed by a pimp to start hooking. When the father heard the pimp had taken his daughter to Toronto, the distraught man went after them without telling anyone at work. By the time he located his daughter, he was in a state of hysteria. He was in the midst of trying to throw the pimp off a balcony when the police arrived.

There is no question this poor man was in acute distress, vulnerable to the same risks as are addicts in the workplace. There are numerous examples of workers whose family situations resulted in their being consistently late or absent, or having huge performance problems at work, including serious accidents, because they were unable to concentrate on what they were doing.

THE COURAGE TO CARE

The name of the workplace addiction education and intervention program my colleagues and I helped develop in the mid 1990's, in conjunction with a joint labor/management Steering Committee, is called *Courage to Care*. We recognize, first of all, that it takes a lot of courage for someone with an addiction to seek help. It also takes a lot of courage and caring by the workplace to decide to do something about this insidious problem.

In workshops with employers and unions, we talk about how easy it is to make the 'problem person' the target or focus of all the attention. When this happens it creates an unhealthy and toxic workplace. Instead of focusing on someone else, we ask people to examine their own enabling behaviors. To what extent have they compromised their personal values? An individual must be willing to say, "If I am really an honest, courageous, and trustworthy person, then I should use these values to guide my decision-making processes."

In our *Courage to Care* training, we suggest that participants make integrity the center of their focus. This is done by demonstrating that behaviors and attitudes need to be consistent with shared values and virtues such as respect, trustworthiness, commitment, courage, honesty, and fairness. It then becomes much easier for individuals, or organizations, when faced with any kind of question, if they ask: *Is it honest? Does it show courage? Is it reasonable, respectful, and fair?* Answering these questions will rule out many possible courses of action and ensures enabling behaviors do not continue.

To insist that someone with a substance abuse problem stop using, or demonstrate responsible behavior is absurd. Addicts will keep doing what addicts do. Having tracked the numbers over many years with the work I've been involved in, I know that less than three percent of visits to the EFAP deal with addiction issues. Very rarely will workers with a serious addiction voluntarily seek help.

So it is imperative to insist on personal responsibility from everyone else, from misguided co-workers who cover up for their friends, to untrained supervisors who tend to ignore problems, to unions who can only think about protecting the job. Finally there are the family members who make the problem worse by calling in sick for the addict, and making excuses time and time again.

Ensuring that supervisors hold employees accountable for their work performance is critical to the success of *Courage to Care*. Supervisors and managers need to know how to talk to someone having problems, and know how to document everything so they can fulfill their job responsibilities properly. Good training is critical, but unfortunately it is often missing.

Unions have to take the stand that they will no longer rush to protect someone who is suspected of using on the job, but also do everything in their power to get that individual the necessary help. My colleagues and I worked with one union that took an unprecedented leadership role by developing their own substance abuse education program for union members and families and, if they wished to participate, company people as well.

We need to create the same cultural shift that occurred with the "friends don't allow friends to drive drunk" campaign. That initiative has been a huge success—most of us don't allow that to happen any more. We need the same kind of shift in our workplaces, so that no one turns a blind eye to someone who is impaired or using on the job.

As a final comment on drugs in the workplace, it's my belief that it is very naïve for a workplace to aspire to be a "Drug Free Workplace." Given that addiction is a disease and some people are genetically predisposed to become addicts, then drugs are going to be used in and around the workplace. The better approach is to accept that to be the case, and then work to create a culture where there is no stigma associated with addiction, and where people are more willing to reach out for help. The objective of a program should be to reduce the negative impact of substance abuse on employees, the work environment, and families. And the workplace needs to provide the infrastructure to ensure an effective continuum of care.

CHAPTER TWELVE

ဆ

ADDICTION, RECOVERY, AND TRANSFORMATION

The law of harvest is to reap more than you sow. Sow an act, and you reap a habit. Sow a habit and you reap a character. Sow a character and you reap a destiny.

James Allen, 1864-1912, Author

Human beings have used drugs for thousands of years. Ancient civilizations were known to use opium, and wine apparently was used at least from the time of the early Egyptians. Medicinal use of marijuana goes back to 2700 B.C. in China. In the 19th century the active ingredients in drugs such as morphine, laudanum, and cocaine were discovered and used freely, completely unregulated and prescribed by physicians for a wide variety of ailments.

Drug addiction has been around as long as addictive substances. And there's no doubt drugs have been devastating individuals, families, workplaces, and communities for generations. The genetic potential for addiction continues to be passed on and children continue to be neglected or abused by drug-dependent parents or family members, continuing the cycle. If this disease were ever to be totally eliminated, the difference it would make in our society would be incredible. Addressing addiction has the potential to transform individuals, families, workplaces, and society.

THE TRANSFORMED INDIVIDUAL

Addiction is a disease of the brain that leaves those who suffer from it morally and spiritually bankrupt. As it progresses, it pulls its victims further down into a black hole, leaving them thinking about and doing things they never thought they were capable of doing. This downward plunge is continually fed by feelings of guilt, shame, and remorse, and it becomes harder and harder to get off the descending elevator. This is their common problem.

I strongly believe that a continuing care program which includes participation in a 12-step program gives a structure in which to talk about and release feelings, and to understand common problems. Practicing spiritual principles (e.g. values and virtues) allows individuals to deepen their recovery and lead happier, more fulfilled lives. This is their common solution.

Working the steps of a 12-step program creates an experience that removes the addict's obsession to use, and it rejuvenates the spirit.

All of the pain and anguish addicts live with, and any defects of character are transformed as addicts develop the ability to more effectively address anything that comes up in their lives, when it comes up. As addicts in recovery grow spiritually, their selfishness and self-centeredness are transformed, and they are in a position to be of service to others.

Becoming a different person requires a conscientious effort that starts with an act of surrender where the addict acknowledges he or she is powerless and can't do it alone. Recovery, then, is a process of coming to believe—believe in a Higher Power that can be called upon for help, believe in one's abilities to have loving, intimate relationships, and believe that a life filled with happiness and abundance without addictive substances is both possible and desirable.

I have witnessed many miracles over the years—individuals who were so far down the road of addiction that people around them felt it would take a miracle for them to recover. But it is in working their recovery that the promise of becoming happy, joyous, and free is realized and the transformation is obvious.

THE FAMILY TRANSFORMS

It can be so exasperating dealing with families who resist doing the work that would help the entire family recover. I can understand an addict's resistance, but it baffles me when families aren't willing to do everything possible to help and to heal. An addict may find recovery for him or herself, but the family has also been dealing with emotional trauma that needs to be healed in a conscientious way.

I look at the chaos I experienced growing up, and the fact that five out of seven in my family ended up struggling with a drug addiction. We suffered terribly as a result of this disease, and yet, with the exception of my sister, we all were able to turn that suffering into something positive and go on to live happy, fulfilled lives. Even my parents found true peace and happiness together before my father passed on.

In my case, even though I had quit drinking and was actively working my recovery, one of my two sons ended up having to deal with addiction. It is my hope that my grandchildren (if I should be so blessed) will have the knowledge and understanding required to help them to avert or address early on this terrible disease that runs in our family.

Certainly, addiction for my immediate family members and for my relatives has been a mixed blessing. While we've dealt with our share of pain, we've come through it having gained more knowledge and understanding about what is important in life.

Just as individuals can find happiness, joy, and freedom in their recovery, so too can families. I have worked with many families where the spouse, the parents, and the children have done most, if not all, of the six things asked of addicts and families, and the dynamics within those families were completely transformed. I'd like to believe this means the next generation and the generation after that will benefit.

TRANSFORMATION OF THE WORKPLACE

My colleagues and I have had the good fortune to implement our *Courage to Care* program in a workplace where the CEO realized that if addiction is an illness, and 10 percent of the population suffered from it, then it would be very foolish to think that the answer was simply to fire people as soon as there was a substance-related performance or safety issue. This CEO was able to see from the beginning the possibility of transforming the workplace culture by proactively addressing substance abuse issues.

When union and management leaders begin to understand that they are dealing with a disease, they are more willing, just like family members, to change their behaviors and take action to change the system. With education and understanding, even the deeply entrenched enabling behaviors and traditional adversarial approaches in the workplace can be changed.

My colleagues and I have implemented workplace-based educational programs for long enough to know that by presenting the right information in the right way to a number of people, we will get individuals coming forward saying, "I need to look at the way I am using alcohol/cocaine/prescription drugs/gambling or whatever, and do something before I get into more trouble."

The workplace starts to see amazing results as people come forward, either voluntarily or as a result of performance issues, and a jointly implemented strategy is in place that includes financial support for treatment and a continuing care program. We've worked with some worksites for several years, where we can see how the success starts to build and the cultural change is unprecedented.

In the process of helping employees and their families find recovery, the workplace finds that not only is it transformed, enjoying a more fair and trusting culture, more harmonious labor relations, and much improved safety performance...it has also saved lives.

TRANSFORMING SOCIETY

The issue of drugs in our communities is so huge, and the scope of it so overwhelming, that my approach has been to adopt the philosophy of the guy who walks along a beach after a powerful tidal wave, throwing one stranded starfish after another back into the sea. When asked why he thinks he can make a difference, when there are literally thousands of starfish to contend with, he responds by throwing another one back in the water and saying, "Well, I just made a difference to that one."

Whether it is only one person, one family, or one work organization, my colleagues and I work with what we can to make a difference wherever possible. We attempted on several occasions to implement our *Courage to Care* program as a community-based process. In theory it sounded good, and I believe fundamentally it made sense, but getting all of the different players and stakeholders, in just one small community, to read from the same page proved too overwhelming for us. The energy and commitment required to make the program work could not be sustained by everyone involved, so in the end we went back to focusing on 'starfish'—individuals, families, and work organizations.

Having said that, when it comes to tackling the issue of drugs and our youth today, I believe we need to look to the old African saying, "It takes a village to raise a child." As the problems with drugs and youth continue to escalate, I believe the plight of these children, who are being seduced into using drugs and/or dealing at increasingly earlier ages, will eventually force the village either to its feet...or to its knees.

Unfortunately, many of the programs geared to young people have failed because the adults involved have been unwilling to look at their own behaviors. As parents, we need to look at the example we set for our children. As a society, we need to provide our youth with challenging opportunities so that they can grow themselves up and experience natural highs, with no need to depend upon drugs to do so.

Governments have to take a much greater role in prevention, intervention, and treatment. If the revenue that governments make from alcohol and gambling was put back into these areas it would make an enormous difference. Governments spend millions on the "war against drugs," but we don't seem to be winning that war. I agree that we need to spend money to curb the sale of illegal drugs on the streets, but ultimately more money needs to be spent on prevention and good treatment strategies.

If we want to gain some control over the disease of addiction, we can start today by focusing on our youth. If we want them to grow and develop in a healthy manner, it is essential to have a connected, caring, values-driven community that understands that addiction is an illness. Everyone—parents, teachers, professionals, community resource services—must work together to support and empower our young people by looking at our common values, and promoting the virtues necessary to realize those values. Each one of us has to look within and understand that the way to change the system starts by changing ourselves.

Instead of focusing on the larger drug problem, we, society, must focus on some basic spiritual principles such as honesty, courage, integrity, and service. Going back to the earlier analogy of the addict in the boxing ring, we don't want to be continually punching and kicking at the drug problem. As well, we need to focus on creating a spiritual healing that will change the culture that promotes drug addiction.

I've seen many in recovery become very different people from what they were as active addicts. I've observed family dynamics change dramatically, as family members deal with their loved one's addiction and heal their own pain. And I've witnessed workplaces transform deeply rooted enabling behaviors to become healthy, caring and effective organizations when substance abuse was handled in a proactive, sensitive way.

Miracles happen when we get out of our own way and surrender to a power greater than ourselves. Finding happiness, joy, and freedom in recovery *is* a very real possibility.

ABOUT THE AUTHORS

Jim Stimson has helped hundreds of people transform their lives from soul-destroying addiction to peace and contentment in recovery. A Registered Social Worker, he has spent more than three decades working in the addictions and recovery field. For two of those decades he ran the Employee and Family Assistance Program for a large international company. Over the years, Jim's work has been widely acknowledged as he's received numerous awards and accolades. He is a highly regarded public speaker and workshop facilitator speaking primarily on the topics of addiction and recovery, and the impact of addiction from the workplace/labor perspective.

Nancy Lee has worked in the communications field for more than 25 years. For 10 years she worked for a large international company (where she met Jim) in corporate communications and for 15 years she has been self-employed managing a variety of projects related to public relations, employee communications, writing, event coordination, and training activities for different clients.

To learn about other recovery tools we've developed, visit our website at www.actofsurrender.com

A portion of the profits from sales of this book will be dedicated to helping families healing from addiction.